Excerpts from this

Everything you do with the rent roll is aimed at determining the truth behind the numbers.

Accomplishing sound financial analysis is predicated on having a solid grasp on actual, delivered rent roll revenue.

The focus of this book is to guide you through a framework to unequivocally capture true contractual rental revenue.

The foundation of rental property ownership is to know what you are purchasing before you purchase it.

When buying a rental property you are in essence buying the rent roll.

Forecasting the value of income property rests squarely on knowing rental income.

The purpose of the rent roll is to act as a current and historic record of rental revenue due based on valid, in-force leases.

A rent roll tells you the amount of contractual rental income you can anticipate for a given period, usually a month. The further reach of a rent roll is to convey in black and white the quality and longevity of projected income.

At the end of the day, under-stating income is reflected in an under-valuation of the asset.

Rent growth measures take into account dramatic occurrences or intentional causes that management or ownership implement.

Knowing rental revenue in its purest form provides you with confidence in the decision to purchase and back-stops your reasoning for buying an income-producing asset.

Identifying average length of tenancy is a significant determinant of resident stability.

Validating rental income is the cornerstone of financial analysis for your income-producing assets.

This publication contains the opinions and ideas of its author and is intended to provide helpful and informative material on the subject of rent roll analysis. It is sold with the understanding that the author and publisher are not engaged in providing accounting, financial or investment advice or any other kind of personal professional services in this publication. The reader should consult their accountancy, legal and other competent professionals before adopting any of the suggestions in this book or drawing inferences from it.

The author and publisher specifically disclaim all responsibility for any liability, loss, or risk, personal or otherwise, directly or indirectly, as a consequence of the use or application of any of the contents of this book.

Copyright 2013

ISBN 0985002735

ISBN e 978–0985002732

Cover and design layout by: Amy Winschel.

How to Read a Rent Roll

A Guide to Understanding ——— *Rental Income* ———

Table of Contents

FREE E–books from the author!

Go to page 159 for the link to download your free e–books today!

For a podcast invitation from the author of How to Read a Rent Roll and an opportunity to participate in free webcasts covering each chapter of the book, please send an email to wecare@rentrolltriangle.com. Each of our podcasts and webcasts are focused on giving you the tools, resources and strategies to read a rent roll with the expertise only available to industry insiders.

About the Author

This long–awaited book by John Wilhoit is the worldwide industry standard on how to review and understand a rent roll. John lays out the history of the rent roll and then dives straight into the components of rent roll analysis. Anyone who has ever tried to get through an article or text book on real estate due diligence will appreciate John's step–by–step method for understanding how to review each piece of the puzzle, and how to get to the truth behind rent roll numbers.

John's approach to rent roll analysis is based on his 20+ years experience working in multifamily asset management and the property management profession. His perspective is further broadened by his experience working in the public sector for federal and state agencies and in asset management for a publically-traded real estate investment trust. As an asset manager and owner–operator of apartments, condominiums and townhomes, John has developed his approach by administrating apartments in 38 states.

His blog, Multifamily Insight, provides John's perspective on the world of multifamily acquisitions, management and investing. To subscribe, go to www.multifamilyinsight.com.

John is co–founder of PowerHour Property Management Leadership Academy and author of Multifamily Insight Volume 1.

You will love John's book and the industry expertise and insight that he shares.

Ernest Oriente – President, PowerHour

Ernest F. Oriente, a business coach and trainer since 1995, and a property management industry professional since 1988, is the author of SmartMatch™ Alliances, the co–founder of PowerHour, PowerHour Leadership Academy and has a passion for creating high leverage alliances for property management teams and their leaders.

Preface

Do you know all the elements of a rent roll? This book is intended for those who are on the verge or in the throes of buying income–producing property. One of your foremost tasks in the acquisitions process is to validate contractual rental revenue. Rental revenue is provided to prospective investors under the terms of a confidentiality agreement. This agreement prohibits you from sharing the information with anyone unrelated to the transaction. The seller will provide you with certain financial data, including the rent roll, for your inspection during the due diligence period. It is up to you to validate this information.

Buying rental property is not an impulse purchase. The acquisition process is a significant time commitment and one that can be very rewarding. As a prospective buyer, you need to know how to build, understand and use the rent roll to your advantage.

This book is a technical guide to rent roll analysis. The objective here is to narrow your attention to one thing and one thing only; estimating the validity, or reliability, of contractual rental revenue collected from income property. Why is this important? Because getting it wrong undermines any and all further work performed towards the goal of estimating Net Operating Income (NOI). If the revenue number is suspect, over–reported, under–reported or credit quality is without support, then what's the point of devoting energy, resources or dollars to completing the rest of the equation towards NOI? Without a solid foundation based on valid rental income the balance of your due diligence is an exercise in futility.

The origins of this book began in Omaha, Nebraska, while enjoying a quiet morning in my hotel room. I opened my laptop with the intention of writing a new blog post for *Multifamily Insight*. The first thing I see is a search term that sent someone to our website: "how to read a rent roll." My post entitled, **"How to Read a Rent Roll – Eight Ways to Sunday,"** is one of the most visited pages on our blog (http://www. multifamilyinsight.net.)

This led me to the idea of conducting an informal review of recent literature related to buying income property. What I found was most surprising! In book after book on the subject very little attention was devoted to the importance of rent roll analysis. I asked myself, *"How can someone write an entire book on buying income property without providing guidance on a review of the rent roll?"* In book after book—to my astonishment—I found absolutely no references to the subject of rent roll in the indexes. Even more puzzling was that in some books there was no mention of rent roll analysis at all. It seemed incredulous, that in book after book on the subject of how to buy real estate for college real estate classes and the general public there was absolutely no mention of **rent roll analysis.** I found myself with a worthy challenge that morning and set out to fill the void on this subject.

Throughout this book you are guided towards creating the paper trail in support of findings from rent roll due diligence. **How to Read a Rent Roll** begins with providing a historic background and purpose for the rent roll, followed by a closer look at its elements. This is followed by a discussion on market analysis, rent and revenue, revenue metrics and rent growth metrics. Next is discovery and methods for documenting revenue, then guidance on high–touch analysis. We also will discuss what to review during a site visit and key factors in determining credit quality. The book concludes with a means for measuring income viability utilizing the Rent Roll Triangle™.

Introduction

"The first casualty of war is truth"
– Senator Hiram Johnson, 1918

Conflict keeps many people from sleeping at night. We live in a world in conflict, from office politics or the constant bickering between the children. We just can't seem to get people to agree. The same holds true for estimating a stated number for contractual rental revenue from income–producing real estate.

What is a rent roll?

A rent roll is the property owner's representation of rental income derived from an income–producing real estate asset.

It's true that buying rental property can sometimes seem like a "shotgun wedding." Everyone is cordial during the courting process, getting to know one another. At the point where the buyer decides to have a relationship with the property—a meaningful, long–lasting relationship—all hell breaks loose. The decision to buy sets off a race to the finish (closing) line. All of a sudden thirty days seems like thirty minutes as due diligence time ticks away at light speed. There are so many things to do! Where's the check–list?

This book will assist you in staying focused on what matters. And what matters most, aside from the going–forward functional life of the asset being purchased, is the quality of the income stream that comes with it.

This book is all about validating and authenticating rental income. My goal is to reduce some of the conflict generated between two or more people, mainly the buyer and seller, when it comes to agreeing on a stated number as represented by the rent roll. Rent roll analysis is the first step in assessing an income–producing real estate asset. Getting this right is imperative, as this number affects every other number in the financial analysis that follows. The best of all worlds is when buyer and seller can agree on the amount of rental income. When a buyer and seller of rental property are on the same page regarding rental income, the potential for conflict decreases exponentially. Less conflict leads to a higher probability of the transaction closing.

According to the IRS, a person or entity who owns an interest in real property meets the criteria in the next paragraph. Try reading this in soft sunlight; otherwise your eyes may feel a burning sensation. The short version of who owns an asset is the party with the rights to the income. Unlike oil wells and commercial default swaps, the line of ownership between the asset and the owner is usually within a stone's throw. Regarding the the IRS version below: Note the tiny print is intentional and, I believe, "government issue" for anything that begins with CFR (Code of Federal Regulations).

Pursuant to 26 CFR 1.856–3 (c) [Title 26 Internal Revenue; Chapter I Internal Revenue Service, Department of the Treasury; Subchapter A Income Tax; Part 1 Income Taxes; Normal Taxes and Surtaxes; Regulated Investment Companies and Real Estate Investment Trusts; Real Estate Investment Trusts], the term Interests in Real Property "includes fee ownership and co–ownership of land or improvements thereon, leaseholds of land or improvements thereon, options to acquire land or improvements thereon, and options to acquire leaseholds of land or improvements thereon.

What this definition really says is "who owns this property is who owns the rent roll and the rights to the income from the rent roll."

This book will greatly assist you in determining one simple answer to the question: what is contractual rental revenue? Aggregate financial analysis is outside of the scope of this book. The reason for this is because without having a very high level of comfort about income the rest of the work, in terms of getting to net operating income, is meaningless. Secondly, there is an on–going presumption that rent roll analysis is easy. The reason rent roll analysis is perceived as easy is that too many people misinterpret the scope. The intention of this book is to ensure that you have the full scope of what the job entails at your disposal. As with so many other aspects of life *there are no short cuts*. This rule applies to rent roll analysis.

The Magna Carta, the English charter of 1215 signed by King John of England, spelled out certain rights including property rights. The Magna Carta is part of the historic record of what became constitutional law that has spread from England to English colonies and beyond. These rights included certain liberties and precluded the King from acting in ways that placed him above the law, such as arbitrarily removing a baron and his family from land owned by the baron.

Historically, a rent roll refers to the amount of rent due from a property. In pre–revolutionary America, these properties were almost exclusively agricultural lands "rented" in exchange for a percentage of crops produced. In other contracts, the rent was a fee paid to the land owner. From 17th century America there are records about tracts of land rented that state the size of the parcel and the rents due to land owners. Often a parcel was known by a name and certain natural divisions (like creeks and rises).

"In America, Sir George Calvert, 1st Baron Baltimore, 8th Proprietary Governor of Newfoundland (1579–1632) was an English politician and colonizer. He achieved domestic political success as a Member of Parliament and later Secretary of State under King James I. Calvert took an interest in the colonization of the New World, at first for commercial reasons and later to create a refuge for English Catholics. He became the proprietor of Avalon, the first sustained English settlement on the island of Newfoundland.

Discouraged by its climate and the sufferings of the settlers, Calvert looked for a more suitable spot further south and sought a new royal charter to settle the region, which would become the state of Maryland. Calvert died five weeks before the new charter was sealed, leaving the settlement of the Maryland colony to his son Cecilius. His second son Leonard Calvert was the first colonial governor of the Province of Maryland. Historians have long recognized George Calvert as the founder of Maryland, in spirit if not in fact." (Wikipedia)

In this lineage, the individual changed over time while the rights, privileges, land and "rent roll" remained with the title. Lord Baltimore was he whom embodied the title by right and by blood. In Maryland during the rule of Lord Baltimore he was the "landlord" of record.

Those charged with collecting rent on behalf of Lord Baltimore were known as rent roll keepers.

"Rent Roll Keepers were responsible for recording information regarding land sales, acreage, and the like, in order to produce an accurate record of rents owed for land owned by Lord Baltimore. Prior to 1707, the task fell variously to the Secretary, or to clerks in each county. The position was divided into two districts in 1733. The position ceased to exist upon the abolition of the quiet–rent system with the advent of the Revolution." Edward C. Papenfuse, et al., Archives of Maryland, Historical List, new series, Vol. 1. Annapolis, MD: Maryland State Archives, 1990.

Rent Roll Keepers were men of position and authority. Two of the first known Rent Roll Keepers were from Maryland; James Carroll in Anne Arundel County, from 1707–1729 and Richard Bennet III in Queen Anne's County, from 1730 to 1733.

How to Use this Book

Validating contractual rental income is the cornerstone of financial analysis for your income–producing assets. Having incorrectly stated rental income skews all of the other percentages and ratios performed thereafter. As a buyer of income property, it is solely your responsibility to validate the numbers. It is your money and your equity that is driving the transaction. Therefore, it is your responsibility to accurately validate rental income through careful examination and due diligence.

This book provides a step–by–step methodology for the review, measurement and validation of contractual rental income from the rent roll for an income–producing property. There are numerous metrics available for the valuation of income property. This book focuses on the rent roll and various means to measure the quality of the income stream derived from the existing, in–place tenant base. The entire exercise of validating income via the rent roll is devoted to determining value. And value is best determined when having a high degree of confidence in the income derived.

This book is about creating a paper trail in support of your findings from rent roll due diligence. In a recent interview, Arthur Levitt, the former chairman of the Securities and Exchange Commission, was asked why certain crimes gain the majority of the agency's attention. Chairman Levitt stated that certain crimes have potential to harm the entire financial system, thereby negatively affecting public confidence and belief in the fairness of the markets. He then gave this example: "It's like a bikini, what a bikini reveals is interesting, but what it covers is <u>essential</u>." In this book we focus on the essential. When buying income–producing assets it is <u>essential</u> that you understand the quality and strength of the income stream being purchased.

Let's assume you are buying what appears to be a solid income property and have it under contract. Two weeks into the due diligence period the seller provides a "revised" rent roll. The numbers are exactly the same as the previous rent roll supplied by the seller. There is just one difference; half the names have changed. What does this mean? What do you do? How do you address this?

The probability is high that the income stream for this asset is far weaker than it appears. By the end of this book you will be able to ascertain with a high degree of accuracy the truth behind the numbers. Knowledge is power and with power comes change. You may change your strike price and be able to share with the seller why you now believe the value has changed, based on your own due diligence. This knowledge will allow you to proceed with the purchase knowing where you stand based on your rent roll analysis.

I have many friends in various aspects of the real estate business, some of whom center their activities exclusively on acquisitions. One of my friends is notorious for saying how much? His question is unrelated to asking price. What he is really asking is, how much income is in the rent roll and is this number valid? Many buyers devote their due diligence to determining Net Operating Income (NOI). My friend targets valuing the quality of the income stream as the front line of attack in determining NOI.

Net Operating Income (NOI) is a most important number. To assure NOI is valid it is important to have a high degree of confidence that rental income is legitimate. The lion's share of revenue from an income–producing asset is rental income. This is where you start on the journey to NOI.

If you devote X number of hours validating rental income, these hours should be delineated based on the source of revenue. And since most income is from rents, we zero in on this source as represented on the rent roll.

Presented throughout this book are focal points for validating a rent roll with an eye towards determining asset stability as represented by Gross Potential Rent (GPR), stated rent, leases and lease terms, and collections. The objective is to provide insight into the stability of an income–producing real estate asset by knowing the financial reality associated with the income stream.

Introducing the Rent Roll Triangle™

This book concludes with a discussion of the Rent Roll Triangle™ (RRT). With respect to rental income, RRT points to actionable areas of concern. RRT localizes problems related to rental income allowing operators (property managers and owners) to address identified issues in real time.

The Rent Roll Triangle™ (RRT) is a simple mathematical calculation to measure the stability of future income based on gross rent potential, stated lease rents, collections and lease term.

The RRT is formulated from three critical data points garnered from the rent roll to evaluate the probability of current income continuing into the future. I anticipate RRT will be a springboard to advances in understanding rent roll analysis for you.

Skipping over the bulk of this book to learn the calculation is discouraged. RRT is simply a mathematical method to view an income–producing asset. Relying on any single calculation to determine value is myopic and potentially costly. To gain the most from this book, an orderly reading of the chapters will deliver the intended precepts as each chapter builds upon the preceding chapter.

Throughout this book you will see the words, "It's your money." This is a reminder that your investment perspective should be the same as a direct investor or as a fiduciary on behalf of others. Treat the money as your own. This frame of thinking will lead you to quality decision making.

Chapter 1: Rent Roll

What is Rental Property?

The payment of rent for use of an item is part of our everyday vernacular. We rent cars, homes, boats, even televisions. An airline ticket can be seen as renting a seat on an airplane to a destination on a particular date and time. Most often, however, a conversation about rent refers to real estate property. The application of this book is best suited to the analysis of rental property. We answer the question about rental property prior to the discussion of rental income because without ownership of rental property you have no rights to the income derived from the property.

Rental property can be inhabited by people, businesses or things. Homes and apartments are rented to people for residential use; malls rent "store fronts" to businesses to sell their wares in exchange for a percentage of revenue; businesses rent warehouses to hold and then distribute their goods. Google® rents buildings for servers. Farmers rent space inside a grain silo to store their crops. Taco Bell® rents land to build their stores on. These are all examples of rental property.

Ownership of rental property is a business. A business opens its doors for purposes of conducting business and making a profit. The property owner sets out a sign selling his or her wares—a certain space for a certain price. For example, to sell space, a purveyor uses a plaque on the door, a sign in the yard, newspaper ads, 365 Connect®, Craigslist®, HotPads®, Zillow®, Trulia®, custom built websites, leasing agencies, housing specialist, rental list and word of mouth.

Rental property is, in its simplistic form, real estate property owned by one person and made available to another person with an exchange of value.

Owners of rental property accept money for the use of a particular space for a set length of time. Most residential property is rented in one year increments with payment of rent due once each month. Commercial, retail and office space is rented in one, three, five and twenty year increments. Hotels rent rooms for one night at a time. These are all forms of rental property.

What is Rental Income?

Rental income is the contractual payment of rent received by owners or owners' representatives from tenants for services rendered. In the case of rental property, the service rendered is having provided (or about to provide) the use of a dwelling or space for a particular period of time for a particular payment, usually measured in money. According to the IRS, rental income is:

"Your gross rental income and all amounts you receive as rent. Rental income is any payment you receive for the use or occupation of property."

Here is another definition:

Rental income is any payment you receive for the use or occupation of property.

One of the oldest forms of rent comes from share cropping. This is when the owner of land grants the use of their land to a farmer to plant a crop. In exchange, the farmer provides a share of the crop to the land owner as rent.

Money for nothing and rent for free. (a song from the band Dire Straits)

The best of all worlds for the land user is a very low payment or no payment to the land owner for use of the land, or in other words, free rent. In modern times, there really is no such thing. If use of the land were provided for free with no rent paid to the land owner there is still a cost associated with its use like taxes and insurance. Thus there is still a cost to pay by someone each and every year. Therefore, when a parcel of land or dwelling is rented and rent is not paid, the landlord is subsidizing the renter by maintaining the taxes and insurance payments even though they receive no remuneration for doing so.

Modern day rent payments are an important component to the workings of our society. In most states, real estate taxes are a very large percentage of local governmental budgets. These tax payments support fire, police and schools. Owners of rental property, in effect, collect some or all of these taxes from users of rental property. Using the term "circle of life" may seem cheesy, but rental property is rented with a portion of rents being circulated into public use funds.

There are occasions in property management when you will have to ask people to leave for non–payment of rent. People provide many reasons why they cannot pay their rent. The universal response to their non–payment could be; "You cannot live here for free because this space can be rented to another who will provide payment." The more in–depth response could be; "Without your payment the owner of this property must continue to pay the mortgage, taxes, insurance, management, general upkeep and capital expenditures. Therefore, the owner requires this space for a paying customer."

Contractual rental income is the single largest component of revenue from rental property. Contractual rental income is the lifeblood of property ownership. Contractual rental income is the source of revenue that allows a property owner to operate and profit from running the business. Therefore, the non–paying tenant must vacate so that the owner may rent this same space to a paying customer.

What is a Rent Roll?

When buying a rental property you are in essence buying the rent roll. Why is it important to establish the amount of monthly income from the rent roll? Because this is the contractual re–occurring revenue established from existing, in–force leases. The rent roll is a snapshot of current income as represented by the owner of the asset.

The rent roll is the property owner's representation of rental income derived from an income–producing real estate asset.

The rent roll is the most critical document in formulating the value of income property. Authenticating numbers on the rent roll leads to creating a high level of comfort in your property buying decision–making process. When considering the acquisition of income property, without discounting the importance of various ancillary income sources, you must devote the most attention to the largest source of revenue, which is the rental income as reflected on the rent roll. A review of each lease file is imperative to validating contractual rental income as reflected on the rent roll. Any number represented on the rent roll must tie to a date and amount as denoted on leases; from rent to late fees to lease term.

Is it true that "if" is the biggest word in the English language? In rent roll analysis, "if" rents collected as described by executed leases matched the rent roll, month in and month out, answering the question about collected rental income is answered. Alas, this is seldom the case. There is no room for the word "if" in due diligence of rental property acquisitions. There is too much money at stake. If (there's that word again) you take this book in earnest, then the money at stake is probably yours. Therefore what you do to acknowledge and address discrepancies between rental income as presented and rental income legally due per the collective leases is vastly important.

A rent roll, correctly assembled, is a distinctive document providing you with an array of information. The rent roll is a snapshot of rents due for the period as reflected in signed and valid leases. The rent roll is utilized by owners, managers, lenders and government agencies as a springboard to understanding the value and stability of a particular real property asset. The rent roll will state the start and end date of the obligation to pay rent, per the terms of the lease.

The rent roll is distinct from a collections report. A collections report conveys the actual amount collected for a given period, usually a single month. The rent roll reflects the stated amount of rent due based on in–place leases. Here are some definitions of a rent roll:

The total income arising from rented property from signed and valid leases.

The property owner's representation of rental income derived from an income–producing real estate asset.

A document showing the rent due, per the lease, and total amount to be received from each tenant.

A list of tenants, usually including the lease expiration date, and rental rate for each one.

A document that reflects the total income as represented by "in–force" leases.

The first definition above is the most accurate representation of contractual rents:

The total income arising from rented property from signed and valid leases.

Now that you know what a rent roll is, you can focus your due diligence time to ensure the information presented is true and correct, valid and enforceable. Everything you do with the rent roll is aimed at determining the truth behind the numbers.

Any and all analysis you accomplish is performed with the intent of validating the income as represented by the seller/owner/owners' representative. That is what you really want to know from the rent roll. You are seeking the actual versus the projected; transparency over trajectory.

Is the rent roll true as represented?

Is the rent roll a fair and accurate representation in form and substance?

I cannot overstate this: Validating rental income is paramount in the financial analysis of an income–producing asset. Having incorrect income skews all of the other percentages and ratios performed thereafter.

In many instances the rent roll is presented as a broker's opinion or that of an accountant or bookkeeper employed by the seller. When buying an income property, the question is: how do you see rental income clearly with the consistent "smoke" of glossy reports, fancy brochures and the deluge of information? The answer is through an independent review of the underlying documentation that supports the numbers presented. In other words; start with the leases and "roll them" into a single document leaving opinions in the dust.

The rent roll is not to be confused with occupancy or collections reports. For a stabilized income property, the rent roll is a reflection of the actual monthly income based (usually) on 12–month leases. A lease file review will determine if leases are in fact 12–months in duration.

A lease of a shorter duration has less value because of the costs to "make ready" the space again and again in shorter intervals. A lease of a longer duration can be a reflection of increased value (a two year lease, for example) if rental increases occur at regular intervals. The length of a lease by itself does not speak to the quality of the income stream. Quality is based on payment record; timeliness and delivery of good funds and term of the lease.

An income/expense statement is a starting point for estimating value. Use the rent roll as a guide to forecasting the validity of rents. One of the first things to review is whether rental income from the income statement matches the rent roll. If not, why not?

Certainly, most deviations between the rent roll and profit/loss statement can be accounted for. But when the numbers begin to widen (large monthly differentials between income statement and rent roll) further explanation is required to address the disparity.

The bottom line is, if the two never match, how do you know which document to believe—the income statement or the rent roll? Further due diligence includes a complete and thorough review of lease files, random conversations with tenants, supervised calls to tenants, etc. These actions are designed to validate rental income

Purpose of the Rent Roll

In the Tom Cruise movie, *The Last Samurai*™, a hobby of one character in the movie is to find the perfect cherry blossom. In the end, he concludes that they are all perfect, just as they are. This is unfortunately not true in rent roll analysis; few are perfect, most are flawed.

The purpose of the rent roll is to act as a current and historic record of rental revenue due the lessor based on valid, in–force leases.

Standing behind this record is the payment history of the residents. It is the tail that wags the dog. The rent roll reports the amount of income you can anticipate for a given period, usually a month. The further reach of the rent roll is to convey in black and white the stability, quality and longevity of projected income.

Most income property is purchased with the intent to own it for a period of time: one year, five years, ten years etc. So while it is important to know the current income, it is equally, if not more important, to understand the viability of the asset and its income stream going forward.

As they say in baseball, catch the ball, hit the ball and throw the ball. A great hitter hits the ball 30% to 40% of the time. When making decisions on placing millions of dollars of equity into millions of dollars of hard assets you must have a perfect record when validating income. Anything less is a financial disaster.

You are looking to see if the monthly income statement matches the rent roll. Restated, the income statement and rent roll should tell the entire world the exact same story. If not, why not? Yes, there will be discrepancies, but differentials should be small and easily explained and documented in notes. If discrepancies are wide, like the proverbial "Mack truck" wide, there is cause for concern and reason to require deeper due diligence to determine actual income.

Many government agencies require a certified rent roll as part of annual monitoring. For government programs the rent roll is delivered as an affidavit about collections. Presentation of an inaccurate rent roll can be considered a criminal act. Following is an example of a document required from an affordable housing program. The manager/owner is required to sign this document on an annual basis with delivery of the rent roll and financials.

"This rent roll is made, presented and delivered for the purpose of influencing an official action of the Department of Housing & Urban Development and may be relied upon as a true statement of the facts contained herein."

In the case of affordable housing, the rent roll is utilized to assure that the correct rental amount is charged to the resident (resident contribution) and to the government agency responsible for payment of rent. For example, a house or apartment rented for $1,000 (be it Section 8, tax credit or some other program) may require a payment of $300 from the resident with the remainder being paid by a state or federal agency. The rent roll is one of the controlling documents in the checks and balances systems to ensure accurate payments from and to all parties to the lease.

Elements of a Rent Roll

One of the reasons for writing this book is to identify a standard approach to rent roll analysis. This single document describes the rental income side of the equation for a property owner, buyer or other interested party. How hard can that be? Apparently it's pretty hard, as there doesn't seem to be a conclusive source to turn to for a straight answer as to what is included on the rent roll.

After developing a standard format for a rent roll, the next stage of discovery is to determine the strength, or quality, of the income stream for the "regular people" (myself included). We, the people, do not have access to rating services like Moody's or Standard & Poors to call on when assessing credit risks.

Consider owners of means; let's say a group of doctors buying a five million dollar asset. Who can they call for a perfected snapshot on strength or quality of income? Their accountant? Other property owners? Aunt Ruth?

To further confuse matters, perform an Internet search on rent roll. Page one results will include real estate related sites and sites for wheels for a car. Did you know you can rent wheels (the part on your car the tires are on)? One prominent company is named Rent Roll and they "rent" wheels so you can roll in style apparently. But I digress. The discussion here is on real estate rental property.

Rental property is real estate property owned by one person and rented to another person.

The software company Real Page® owns the domain name rentroll.com. Now that makes sense. Their entire business is exclusively providing property management software to rental property owners large and small. The folks at Real Page absolutely know the elements of a rent roll.

There is one particularly authoritative source on the matter of what belongs on a rent roll: Fannie Mae. Along with Freddie Mac, these two GSE's (Government Sponsored Enterprises) provide the bulk of mortgage insurance in the United States.

While these GSE's may not originate many mortgages, they do end up either buying or insuring a large percentage of mortgage industry production. Because of this, they get to call the shots in terms of underwriting. Meet or exceed underwriting standards and approval is probable. Attempt to shortchange the process or only complete the required documentation in part, and your loan application is doomed.

The Fannie Mae rent roll matters because they are the ones with the money. Fannie Mae's "Project Rent Roll Form" starts the ball rolling.

Following is an excerpt from *Instructions for Completing the Certification to Project Rent Roll (Form 4243) and Exhibit A*:

"The Borrower must provide a copy of the property's rent roll to be submitted as Exhibit A to Form 4243. The rent roll can be submitted in one of two formats: the Borrower may utilize the Exhibit A template attached to this form for rent roll submission or the Borrower may provide a computer printout in lieu of transferring the individual lease data to the sample Exhibit A."

You think that was exhausting, try reading the full set of instructions! A web search will net you the document for printing and review. Search for "Project Rent Roll Form 4243".

Completing a commercial mortgage application can be an arduous task. Completing a mortgage application that requires GSE approval adds additional layers (i.e., time, expertise, focus, concentration…did I mention time?) to the process. Getting it right opens the door to low-cost, long-term financing. This holds true for most rental assets. The ability to obtain long-term financing makes deals happen. So here we are, back to elements of the rent roll.

If you could have only a single document to convey the financial viability of an income-producing asset, most would elect for a profit and loss (P&L) statement. I agree. When it comes to verifying the rent and revenue represented on the P&L, what is the best information source? The rent roll. A complete rent roll. What is a complete rent roll?

While every income property mortgage isn't underwritten by Fannie Mae, most mortgage lenders follow a similar flight plan. Form 4243 has fourteen (14) elements. The elements of a Form 4243 rent roll are:

- Unit number

- Unit type

- Square footage

- Resident name

- Monthly contract unit rent

- Monthly ancillary income stated in lease

- Written lease inception date

- Written lease expiration date

- Value of subsidy

- Rent net of subsidy

- Value of cash concessions

- Reason concession given

- Utilities included, yes or no

- Delinquencies

Performing rent roll analysis requires, at a minimum, the following data points:

- Unit number or address (street address)

- Unit Type (residential, commercial, retail)

- Name of lessee (marked as vacant if vacant)

- Square feet per unit (rentable square feet)

- Monthly contract unit rent

- Lease start date

- Lease end date

Rent roll analysis requires access to original leases to confirm these data points. With these seven data points you can now begin the process of breaking down the numbers.

I have excluded ancillary (or other income) as they vary widely in their use and revenue generation. There is a discussion about ancillary income later in this book. While not to be excluded in a review of the property financials, the present focus is just rents for purposes of nailing contractually–consistent, reoccurring income.

The foundation of rental property ownership is to know what you are purchasing, preferably before you purchase it. The fewer surprises the better post–closing. The glide path to acquiring a quality rental property begins with successfully understanding the quality of the income stream being purchased, or, understanding the rent roll.

In this chapter we have established clear definitions for rental property, rental income and the rent roll, and expressed the purpose of the rent roll and its elements. With this knowledge you are now prepared to take a closer look at markets, submarkets, rents, competitors and the people who pay rent.

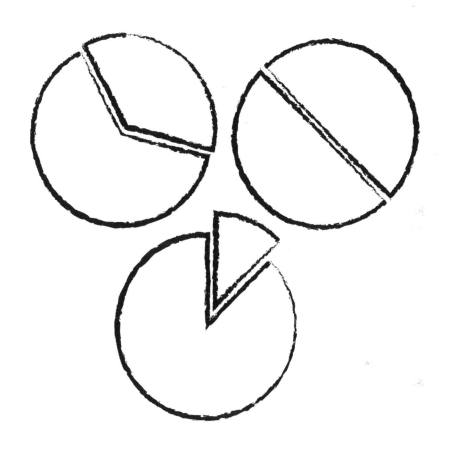

Chapter 2:
Market Analysis

Every rental property is in a market. A market is represented by boundaries that establish the area where a property competes. Each market has competitive properties, such as other entities vying for the same business as the rental property you own or are considering buying. Before looking more closely at individual assets, this chapter paints a broad brush stroke about the place where a property competes, specifically, the market and submarket. In this chapter we also explore how to obtain Gross Potential Rent as a marker of highest revenue. The discussion includes competitive assets and what to look for and what questions to ask. The chapter closes with an extended discussion on demographics. Demographics define attributes about the people that reside in and around a property.

What is a Market?

A market is the place where a rental property must compete represented by established boundaries. A market represents a place and its surrounding infrastructure including physical, social and cultural places. A market represents a place where people live, work, worship and go to school. It is an aggregate location with a certain cohesiveness. New York is a market yet it has five distinct boroughs. Markets represent a political, cultural and economic entity. A market is a place where people "self–identify" with the location and its perception of self. These established boundaries can move over time as properties age, demographics change and new competition enters and exits the market.

A market is the place where a rental property must compete.

While location is a large component in the rental property buying decision, it is by no means the sole decision point. What surrounds a rental property is just as important as the building(s) itself; this includes the people (their average age, income and educational level), businesses and competitive assets. A market is further defined by a polygon that includes the subject property and directly competitive properties. A polygon is nothing more than a boundary. What makes

29

polygons interesting is building them accurately to fit the market area for a property.

Making a determination within a market about population growth and income and aligning this information with the number of rental housing units presently in the market, along with information on housing starts, will provide guidance of future vacancy and rent growth. All of these factors have significant impact on value as higher rent growth leads to higher value.

Submarkets

Once a submarket is geographically defined, a property owner or management company can obtain a very solid view of the population, income and competitive properties affecting an asset. Seldom is this area square or round. Nor does the shape or size follow census tracts or block groups. The shapes, sizes and area covered varies immensely.

A submarket is a geographic area defined by streets, natural barriers and competitive properties.

The money is in the submarkets. Rent growth projections are submarket specific and affected most directly by the number of existing and proposed housing units in an area. Rent growth is directly correlated to availability (in the competitive niche), population and income (both per capita and household income). But population and income growth where?

The where is in the submarket that a rental property competes for residents. The area is defined by competing properties with similar attributes located in the same market and submarket and the demographic attributes of the people living there. The number of existing and proposed housing units in an area and their impact on rent growth is directly correlated to population and income within the submarket.

Market Rents

To obtain accurate numbers in the metrics that follow presumes you have a good handle on market rents within the established boundaries of the market. Guessing market rents brings every other calculation directly into a tailspin. Market rents must be based on real time and accurate information. Here is a definition of market rents:

Market rent is the maximum rent obtained by a lessor in a competitive market.

Here is another definition:

Market rent is the rent that a comparable space will obtain if offered in the competitive market.

How do you determine market rents? The first step is to define the market and as noted above, the submarket. Markets are distinguished by size and quality (size does not always equate to quality, of course).

Here are some examples of market size specifications that assist in defining market boundaries:

- Population and population density

- Population of the market

- Population of the submarket

- Total number of housing units in the market

- Total number of housing units within the submarket

- Total number of rental units in the market

- Total number of rental units within the submarket

Gaining insight on market rents requires knowing precisely which competitive properties your asset is competing against for residents.

Here are some examples of asset quality specifications:

- Quality of construction

- Age and condition

- Property amenities and services

- Is the asset managed professionally?

- Overall upkeep–property presentation

Compare the subject asset to competitors within established market boundaries using these attributes as a starting point to identify directly competitive properties.

The U.S. Department of Housing and Urban Development (HUD) provides some guidance on market rents referred to as fair market rents (FMR) (see http://www.huduser.org/portal/datasets/fmr.html). The rents provided are indicative of the particular city named only insofar as the properties described offer housing to the broadest possible population base. From the HUD website, here is a partial definition:

"FMRs are gross rent estimates. They include the shelter rent plus the cost of all tenant–paid utilities, except telephones, cable or satellite television service, and internet service. HUD sets FMRs to assure that a sufficient supply of rental housing is available to program participants. To accomplish this objective, FMRs must be both high enough to permit a selection of units and neighborhoods and low enough to serve as many low–income families as possible."

The FMR standard measure has only limited use for market rate rentals because, as noted above, FMR has a completely different format than that utilized by most property owners as most are not marketing rental housing to income restricted tenants. Market rents are determined by asset competitiveness, not by FMR.

Gross Potential Rent (GPR)

Gross Potential Rent (GPR) is not market rent. GPR represents a perfect world where every rentable square foot is 100% occupied at real time market rents all of the time with never a single day of vacancy for any reason. GPR is a marker of the highest attainable rent. GPR also presumes 100% collections for the entire term of the lease. This is utopia for the owner of any income property. There are caveats even with this number to avoid the smoke and mirrors. The basis for this number, Gross Potential Rent, represents current market rent with zero vacancy. Again, that means never a day of vacancy. Current rents means rents in effect on a real time basis. This leads us right back to the rent roll.

Gross Potential Rent is a present day representation of current market rents with perfect occupancy, collections and continuous real time market pricing.

Regardless of in–place rents, with active property management GPR is regularly updated to reflect rental income potential. One example is when purchasing a "value add" deal. The property is known to need significant upgrades, so much so that the buyer will likely not renew any in–places leases and empty the property for rehabilitation.

Post rehabilitation, the owner is anticipating bringing all rents up to present day market rent. Then the cycle begins again, where with every turnover, or vacancy, all units are presumed to have the possibility of being rented at the same rate as the last unit rented, or higher, based on real time market pricing. Again, you have a new GPR.

In this example, a key determinant of asset purchase price will be GPR post rehab. As a buyer you must now determine with a high degree of accuracy, what the units will rent for post rehab. Knowing rehabilitation costs and GPR you can make an informed decision on what you are willing to pay for the asset given its condition, investors risk appetite and yield requirements.

Gross Potential Rent is the total of all potential rental revenue from an income property (office, industrial, retail or multi–family) assuming collection of rents from all existing tenants and assuming collection of market rent values on all vacant leasable space. From HUD:

Gross potential rent (GPR) is the projected income of a project assuming all units are occupied at all times. GPR represents "real time" rental rates for all space in a building.

The formula: Total current market rents attainable, including an imputed number for all vacant space, for the most recent period. If you are using the monthly total, then multiply by twelve. This annualized number represents annual Gross Potential Rents.

Example: One hundred units rent for $900 each. The formula presumes that each rental unit is occupied with a paying resident for 365 days with no downtime, no days vacant and 100% collections for the entire year. In other words, nirvana. Using this metric GPR = $1,080,000 annually (100 units X $900 per month X 12 months).

In reality, there is vacancy, turnover and days with units off line for various reasons.

Comparable Properties (Comps)

Comps refer to comparable properties. A review of comparable properties in the same submarket as the asset under consideration is imperative. It is important that someone from your team (or you) go see, in person, on foot, these comparable assets. NO driving by. NO pulling down photos from the internet. Go see, go touch the competition. If the acquisition candidate has all new stainless steel appliances and the competitors believe "avocado green" is still in fashion…there's only one way to find out. Go see the properties.

Comparable properties must be within the same market. Market studies often have nice and neat one, three and five mile rings around a star that depict the subject property. For housing, the true market area, the area from which a property draws resident, is seldom a 360 degree sphere. There are always barriers that define the shape as something other than round. These barriers are defined by various aspects. There can be physical barriers such as a freeway; cultural constructs like the local art scene; and financial considerations, such as price or income.

What you are really looking to confirm or deny with a review of comparative assets is if properties within close proximity to the subject asset are in fact in the same value range. Keep in mind that a rental at $500 monthly is not competing against a rental of $2,500 monthly, even if they are within close proximity. Once you have identified those that are comparable then you can review both the asking and actual rents on an apples–to–apples basis.

If there are a significant number of similar attributes, and if the subject property and comparable properties are in the same market and have many of the same attributes then the competitive asset is probably an acceptable comparable property. A more simplistic way to determine competitiveness is to determine if the properties are competing for the same residents. In car sales, for example, Nissan and Toyota compete head–to–head. Neither brand is competing with Ferrari or Rolls Royce.

When selecting competitive assets within close proximity and of similar age, for the subject asset and competitive properties, identify and collect these data points for comparison:

- Asking rent per square foot

- Actual rent per square foot for similar quality space

- Street level visibility (car counts)

- Comparative amenities

- Access and availability to parking

- Incidents of crime

- Age of asset

- Amenities (pool, clubhouse, fitness center, landscaping, ambiance)

- Proximity to jobs, schools, shopping and medical

- Number of bathrooms per unit

- Similar unit sizes

- Current concessions offered

With this you can begin to gather rent prices per square foot and look at relative rents and values.

How does this fold into rent roll analysis?

When you have determined which apples are comparable to your apple, you can further deduce if presented rents are real, or comparable to market rents for the subject property. How? Shop them as described above. Call and go see competitors. Become a renter and go visit. Talk to current tenants. Purchase local newspapers and review local media. Call leasing offices, and on–site and off–site leasing offices. Talk to Realtors. And lastly, use on–line resources including social media, Craigslist® and apartment review sites. The best method to review comps is to physically walk onto the grounds of the comparable properties.

Knowing floor plans and amenities, having defined the market and shopped the competition, you will have determined market rents... all by yourself. No relying on a reliable source or guessing based on a single set of data.

Some assume the average market rent t is a good starting point. Not true. With every asset there are always some distinguishing features to differentiate the space. Properties compete against other properties in the marketplace acknowledging this differentiation. Yet, there is still a price set for each and every available space. An assessment assist in explaining the reasoning behind the differentials. By knowing the facts behind the numbers you can compete more effectively against direct competitors.

One criterion to assess comparative assets is to evaluate those that provide the same level of property management the subject property provides or intends to provide. Professional property management can realize extreme advantages over non–professionally managed assets. If the subject asset is presently not being professionally managed and you intend to employ professional management post acquisition, factor this into the pre–acquisition equation; management expense should appear as a line item on the pro forma profit/loss with expectations of operational improvements based on professional management.

Demographics

While location is a large component in the real estate buying decision, it is by no means the sole decision point. A property's locale or environment is just as important as the building(s) itself. Using public information, about populations such as average age, household income and educational attainment, you can identify a number of data points that assist in forecasting the relative financial strength of an area. These three factors provide good qualitative information about a market, neighborhood or submarket. Financial data alone is a single data point representing the value of an asset. The determinant of real value is in understanding current and future utilization...and by whom. The "whom" is identified by demographic and market analysis.

Following are data points that can aid in providing a "sense of place." Of course, for a place you've never heard of or seen, this data alone is not sufficient for making investment decisions. However, these factors will significantly enhance your location specific knowledge, including for places you *think* you know well.

Census Data. The volume of information provided by United States Census Bureau can easily create that deer–in–the–headlights feeling. Go to: http://www.census.gov/acs/www/. Start with the home page and go to the Data tab, then go to American Community Survey. Here you will find snapshot data on any community without having to dive into the entire website. The Survey provides a starting point for obtaining demographic data for an area.

Traffic patterns. The State DOT (Department of Transportation) can tell you where auto traffic is flowing. Metairie, Louisiana is a place I lived for a year. Pre–Katrina, in 2005, Metairie was poised for growth. Significant retail development was underway and road construction, including an expansion of interstates, was rolling. I mean, they were loaded for bear!

Let's say you were to review the population data for New Orleans today, pre– and post–Katrina. The data will reflect that auto traffic dropped off a cliff. Why is this important? Because tracing traffic volume and traffic patterns allows you to draw some conclusions and make predictions about future occurrences of population and rent growth based on this information.

When assessing a rental property acquisition target, if the car count has dropped in recent years from, let's say 9,000 cars a day to 3,000 cars per day, there is a reason. The "why" is the question. Large retail chains thrive on this data. Wall Street wants to know year–over–year "same store sales. Sales are based on traffic, both foot traffic and car traffic. In this respect, there is a correlation between retail and rental property.

Building Permits. City/County Planning & Zoning. P&Z knows where builders are going to build even before the builders do. They

38

track not only all the paper related to building, but also planned utilities construction.

When a builder pulls a permit, they are committing real dollars to development and they have likely already made an investment in, architecture and engineering services. They have also confirmed availability of water and electrical service. A builder pulling a permit intends to build.

Within a Census Tract, an over–lay of permits pulled and population growth can point an investor toward knowledge of construction trends and anticipated growth. There is no reason to buy in an area where builders have gone wild at the same time the population is shrinking. Stay away. Stay far away.

Chamber of Commerce. The local Chamber has their hand on the pulse of the business community. It is their job to promote the community to the outside world. They know where development is occurring and who is shipping jobs into and out of the community.

Earlier this decade, in a very short period of time, there was a flood of apartment developments for sale in Hazelwood, Missouri. A little digging found that the Ford Motor plant in that community was closing and with it thousands of jobs were leaving the area. Always check with the Chamber to see who is coming and going.

FBI Statistics. While this information can be daunting, it is important. It's also public information. For a market area, focus on patterns of crime against people and property. What is the direction of the crime trends? Look at violent crime and rape. It's difficult to think about, much less to study. But wouldn't you prefer to know the trends prior to making a buying decision rather than after the fact?

New York City in the 1980□s had terrible crime. Yes, there is still crime there today, but not nearly to the extent as years ago. This single fact has enhanced not only the standard of living in the city, but has had a positive impact on property values.

The Street Cop. These hard–working folks are your best source of on–the–ground information. They are honest reporters. Walk into the local precinct or police station and ask to speak with the officers who cover the area you have an interest in. If the officers are not available or too busy, come back later or make an appointment (remember: their shift and workload is not based on your availability). Police officers are patrolling the very streets you have an interest in buying rental property and they know these streets. Do not discount this.

Professional demographic analysis is very expensive. The methods presented here are not a substitute for professional market studies. The larger the investment, the more necessary professional market surveys become. The preceding is not a substitute for a quality market study or in–depth due diligence.

Following is some demographic vocabulary that will come up in any conversation that has real estate and populations in the same sentence. It's important to know this vocabulary as a foundation to understanding the importance of demographic trends to real estate valuations.

Block Group. Block Groups generally contain between 600 and 3,000 people, with an optimum size of 1,500 people. The census block group is the smallest unit of geography for tabulated Census data.

Census Tract. A census tract is a small geographic area. The primary purpose of census tracts is to provide a nationwide set of geographic units that have stable boundaries. Census tract numbers are unique within a county. A census tract will have from 1,500 to 8,000 persons with the optimal number being 4,000 persons.

Metropolitan Statistical Area (MSA). Careful selection of MSAs can greatly decrease the probability of making an inferior investment. A metro area contains a core urban area of 50,000 or more population. A micro area contains an urban core of at least 10,000 (but less than 50,000) population.

Each metro or micro area consists of one or more counties and includes the counties containing the core urban area, as well as any adjacent counties that have a high degree of social and economic integration as measured by commuting to work with the urban core (www.census.gov/).

Primary Market. These are markets with over one million people in the MSA with all the amenities of a big city from airports (usually plural) to cultural access and cross–industry jobs. They are well defined, well known and have a cultural identity. These are big cities with big city sports teams, 14 Olive Gardens and multiple high–end steak restaurants, multiple freeways and job centers. Examples: Philadelphia, Boston, New York, Chicago, Los Angeles.

24–hour Cities. 24–hour cities have thriving downtowns and never–say–sleep districts. Examples: New Orleans, Atlanta, Chicago, Miami, San Francisco. Note that 24–hour cities are often known by their name alone or by just their airport code: SFO, MIA, and ATL. We distinguish 24–hour cities from primary markets because not every primary market is a 24–hour city.

Secondary Market. Secondary markets are smaller than primary markets but with similar synergies sized to the population. They are usually self–sustaining, but without the expansiveness and do not possess the cultural heritage of primary cities. They may have a single professional sports team, or multiple farm teams. They will have a single primary commercial airport. Examples: Omaha, NE; Birmingham, AL; Little Rock, AR; Oklahoma City, OK; Nashville, TN.

Tertiary Market. These markets may be in the sphere of influence of a primary or secondary market, but based on size and distance, they are dependent on a sister city or nearby metropolitan area. Many have small airports, but it is common for people to fly into the larger airport in a close–by city and drive to the tertiary locale. Examples: Waco, TX; Savannah, GA; Topeka, KS.

Frontier Market. These markets are further from primary and secondary cities than tertiary markets. Reviewing property in frontier markets requires local market expertise as they are often excluded from industry reporting data. These places are just "not on the map" from an institutional buyer's perspective. They are the job center for their area and possess solid community endeavors, and will likely have a small commercial airport. Examples: Dubuque, IA; College Station, TX; Bloomington, IL.

Market and demographic analysis allows you to have a high level of confidence in the Gross Potential Rent numbers generated. Knowing your markets, knowing the demographic profile of residents and potential residents will allow you to compete more effectively. As one of my friends would say, it's part of your "secret sauce" to beating the competition.

Chapter 3:
Rental Revenue

What is Revenue?

Revenue is cash collected from contractual rents and all other sources derived from rental property. Revenue is income received on behalf of the property from normal business activities and placed in a bank account established for that property. Rental property ownership allows for access to revenue sources beyond "just rents.". In some instances, revenue from sources other than rents can be huge. Documenting revenue is discussed in greater detail later in this book. The objective here is to establish a definition and to place revenue in context.

Revenue is the total income produced by a given source, a property expected to yield a large annual revenue (Merriam Webster)

Here is another definition:

That which returns, or comes back, from an investment; the annual rents, profits, interest, or issues of any species of property, real or personal; income. (BrainyQuote)

Note that until revenue is received, it is not income. For purposes of your analysis, income represents revenue received and recorded in a valid bank account held on behalf of the asset.

Everyone—bankers, mortgage companies, your insurance company, the property assessor—wants to know your revenue. Just about every metric you perform is a derivative of revenue (which includes rents). You must know revenue to ascertain common financial outputs. For example, what are expenses as a percentage of revenue?

Another example: What is insurance expense as a percentage of revenue? This is a simple question to answer with good records for revenue and annual insurance premiums. This is important to know because different regions of the country apply different rates based on property type and area claims activity.

It is necessary to have access to multiple years of income and expense records as these records allow you to identify variances and ask questions about identified differentials. With insurance, for example, if premiums have a 20% year–over–year variance you would want to know why, yes?

Bottom line is that most revenue is from rents. You want to see that all revenue sources are collected and deposited for tracking in some form of electronic system, something like QuickBooks® (http://www.quickbooks.com) or via a property management software system.

Revenue refers to ordinary income from operations and excludes extraordinary events such as insurance settlements. Revenue is gross income derived from operations. Extraordinary events must be accounted for, but cannot be presumed as re–occurring. Property owners do not count on making money from insurance claims or lawsuits.

Income received from a source other than an existing resident may represent income, but is excluded from the rent roll unless it is deemed rental income. Why? Because revenue other than rental revenue is not obtained under the contractual terms of the lease.

For the moment, let's avoid the rabbit hole. Regarding non–rental revenue, generally speaking, it is hard to make someone use on–site laundry if they choose to go elsewhere (it's a free country after all). As for late fee revenue, most residents avoid them if at all possible. So these sources of revenue, while important and measurable, are by their very nature variable. They are important because, collectively, non–rent revenue can sometimes represent 10% of revenue. Although that's a big number it will never attain the importance of rent. Remember that variable revenue is not contractual revenue.

Revenue Recognition

Revenue recognition is an accounting principle under generally–accepted accounting principles (GAAP) that determines the conditions under which income becomes realized. Generally, revenue is recognized only when a fundamental event has occurred (like a deposit) and the amount of revenue is measurable from formal records (such as bank statements and tax returns). Formal revenue recognition records income during the period in which it is earned rather when it is received.

This is not an accounting book nor do we wish to provide accounting advice. Most people in business know there are two primary ways to book income: cash basis and accrual basis. The revenue recognition principle:

...requires that revenues be shown on the income statement in the period in which they are earned, not in the period when the cash is collected. This is part of the accrual basis of accounting as opposed to the cash basis of accounting (www.accountingcoach.com)

Read more at: http://www.investopedia.com/terms/r/revenuerecogntion.asp#ixzz1iozUAyuH

Most income property owners book income upon receipt, making revenue recognition immediate and confirmed by deposit receipts and bank statements. High value commercial assets, having more complex lease structures and depreciation schedules, are very selective in the manner in which they book income.

Collected vs. Contractual Rental Revenue

Completing a real estate transaction can be an arduous task. There are numerous moving pieces and many metrics to measure—beginning with determination of contractual rental income, a focal point of this book. Estimating the value of income property rests squarely on *knowing* contractual rental revenue. Contractual income seldom aligns precisely with collected income. You must know contractual income to ascertain what the property should be collecting. The next task is to confirm that collected income equals contractual income.

Knowing contractual rental revenue in its purest form provides confidence in your buying decision and back–stops your reasoning for buying an income–producing asset.

In rent roll analysis your constant question is: Does collected income equal contractual income? This review of the rent roll is a guide to estimating future rents. The review includes verification that contractual rental revenue from the income statement matches collected income as reflected on the rent roll. If not, why not?

Practically every other number you produce in the review of an asset ties back to *knowing* contractual rental revenue. The magic number, the objective of all of your efforts in rent roll due diligence is to know actual rental revenue from the preceding 12–months of operations. Knowing this strips away distractions.

Collected Rental Revenue – Magic Number #1 (T12)

Beginning with the most recent full prior month rental revenue and building the trailing 12–months income (T12) provides a one–year snapshot of collected rental income. This data is the baseline for extending due diligence further. Resolving 12–month trailing income is a cornerstone for future assumptions when analyzing income property.

In your review of the rent roll, determine the amount of rental revenue received for the most recent full calendar month and then extend this (with documentation) to include the most recent previous 12–month period, often referred to as the "trailing twelve," resulting in the previous 12–month rental revenue. This is expressed as "T12".

This revenue from the rent roll, referred to as the Trailing Twelve, is the trailing 12–months of "collected" rental income. It is a representation of revenue received—not booked or credited, but income banked, collected, or accountable in transferable cash obtained by the property.

Minus the layered view of revenue including Gross Potential, less vacant, less concessions, plus ancillary income the question is; how much rental revenue was collected for the current month versus for the same month one and two years prior? You need this number to establish a trendline.

Accomplishing sound financial analysis is predicated on having a solid handle on actual, delivered rent roll income. The point of rent roll analysis is to deliver a believable number on rents into the mix of the next step of property analysis, which is to determine NOI.

- What were collected rents one year prior?

- How many tenants remain from one year earlier?

- What is the amount of rent growth from the existing resident base, year–over–year?

It is imperative to have an historic perspective of current rental revenue as described by, for example, an aged rent roll for the subject asset. Just like Wall Street analyses is performed on every Fortune 500 company, you want to know what the rental revenue is in this period as compared to the same period one year earlier. Building a trendline requires two or more years of data.

Net Operating Income – Magic Number #2

It may seem as if NOI is a stepchild in this book. It would be so easy to veer off the rent roll road and dive into the deep pool of NOI losing focus from the rent roll. But, while NOI is all important, NOI will never be accurate without having a solid handle on actualized rental income. Therefore, your eye must remain firmly on rent roll analysis.

But make no mistake, all of your work here leads to the generation of high quality outputs when the time comes to produce NOI numbers.

Net Operating Income is the income remaining after payment of operating expenses.

As owners or buyers of income property, your two–pronged approach to improving operations in any market conditions is to grow revenue and control expenses (G.R.A.C.E). Attacking this requires knowing the real time numbers as they are today. The starting point of attack is having an accurate rent roll.

Your starting point is the rent roll. The second step is to determine NOI. The focus of this book is to guide you through a framework to unequivocally capture true contractual rental income. Once accomplished, getting to NOI is a very satisfying exercise because of the high level of validity established from the rent roll.

Appraisals

In the appraisal business, there are three main valuation methods: replacement value, the income approach and market approach. Market valuation relies most heavily on numbers generated from the rent roll. Unfortunately, for people attempting to obtain comparative numbers for determining value prior to obtaining an appraisal, you are on your own or worse, having to rely on people with whom you have no prior relationship for good numbers.

Think of an appraisal as a professionally prepared document that validates the valuation you (the potential buyer) have determined. This may sound egotistical. I am not suggesting that your determined value is better than one produced by a professional appraiser. However, your selected strike price is the number you must be willing to live with in terms of a purchase price. After all..it's your money. A quote from Jerry Seinfeld:

"You go and watch a bad movie, it's two hours out of your life. I go and make a bad movie, it's two years out of my life."

The reason your number has significant merit is because it is your money that is being committed to an investment for an extended period—much longer than a two hour movie. The appraiser has no money at risk. Appraisers have a business to run; they follow a professional code of ethics, and they have a reputation to protect. When the appraisal is over, however, they go home. If you buy the asset in question the journey has just begun. Therefore, your opinion of value has great authority...because it is your money.

When reading a commercial appraisal (and who wouldn't love to spend an afternoon combing through the footnotes) there will be a list of documents the appraiser refers to in reaching his or her conclusions on value. These documents are referred to as evidentiary documents. They represent the data points in the appraisal toolbox that they point to as evidence of sound due diligence as a requisite in presenting the valuation decision expressed in the appraisal report.

As so much is riding on that eventual number, every interested party wants assurances that the appraisal is based on sound and professional standards. Aye, but here's the rub: The list of evidentiary documents seldom includes a review of the in–place lease files. Is the rent roll requested? Yes. Is the rent roll validated? No. From the checklist of requested evidentiary documents from an unnamed appraiser, Item # 9 is:

Rent roll showing apartment numbers and dates of leases, and the type of apartment, and the contractual rent for each apartment unit.

Really? That's all you want? What about a review of the actual lease files to see if real people have signed real lease agreements? In defense of appraisers, they would suggest that the lease is a single source of information in the valuation process and that their overall investigation in valuing an asset relies on a scope beyond the lease agreements. I recommend performing a review of 100% of the lease files. As I've said before, "It's your money."

Property Management

Rental properties do not manage themselves. Maximizing revenue requires the implementation of professional expertise applied to the assets under management. There is no such thing as hands–free management of rental property. If you want to own real estate that is on "auto pilot," buy a real estate related stock. That way you are buying a very small portion of an asset pool that is professionally managed.

Maximizing revenue requires professional property management. A small property owner will often consider self–management under the auspices of "How hard can it be?" They read a book or two (or not) and assume that property management will be a part time gig they can squeeze in around their already busy lives. This is seldom the case. A property, even a small one, does not care about your busy life. It has needs that seldom fit into a time slot selected by the part–timer.

Professional property managers are in the customer service business. We all have our favorite coffee shop. How long until you find a different favorite place if "Grumpy" takes your order every day? Probably not long. Property management professionals are the front line to your potential customers and the receipt of revenue. Managers are at their best when they are authentic, not wearing their feelings on their sleeve, being professional and engaging. In short, offering consistent service to esidents leads to higher NOI.

Building NOI requires quality management. Residents absolutely need their relationship with the property manager to work. Otherwise, they can move elsewhere, seeking a place to live with a good relationship with management. This cannot be underestimated.

Quality property management interaction with your residents makes for a higher probability of a long–term relationship with each of your residents. Longer relationships equate to less turnover. Lower turnover equals a more predictable revenue number on the rent roll and higher NOI.

In exchange for their service, the property manager earns a fee. This fee is paid from rental revenue. The incentive, , for the property manager to maximize revenue is that their fee is a percentage of revenue collected. More revenue, higher fees are paid. They are incentivized.

Small property owners will say, "I cannot afford a property manager." I submit if this same owner will convert the amount "saved" as compared to the time they devote to management, then this owner is probably working for minimum wage. The professional property manager is working at a higher rate of pay because of their increased efficiency over the untrained part–timer.

To property owners large and small who are not full–time in the real estate business, I strongly suggest you engage professional property management. Here are some of the benefits of professional property management:

- Leasing

- Collections

- Expert systems

- 24–hour emergency response

- Vendor relationships

- Owner reports

- Maintenance staffing

Professional property management pays for itself with higher revenue. So regardless of the asset class and size, unless you are personally willing to address the items mentioned above, consider hiring expertise (read: professional property management) for the day–to–day operations of your rental property.

A note on having family members as managers. This is seldom a good idea. When an extended family is purchasing an asset, the individual with the most money in the deal controls the deal. So if Auntie, with the most equity in the property, wants to hire an unemployed nephew as manager, nephew is usually hired, right? The size and complexity of rental property suggests that whoever is hired brings a certain minimum level of skills by having operated a property of similar size regardless of ownership structure. So interview potential candidates, including property management companies. Regardless of the person or entity hired, the interview process will allow everyone to recognize that management options are available beyond family members.

Having concluded this discussion on rental revenue, next up is an exploration of rent growth metrics and the calculations that allow you to compare year–over–year operational numbers for any rental property in review, comparing and contrasting comparative properties.

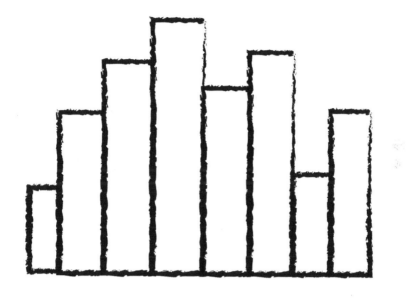

Chapter 4:
Rent Growth Metrics

Rent growth is not to be confused with rental increases. This is a BIG "Y" in the road. Rental increases provide for rent growth, yes. However, rent growth measures extend beyond increases in rent. The reason for recognizing each as a separate measure is because of how the outputs are reviewed and the timing of each event.

Rental increases occur systematically in stabilized assets not experiencing any significant upgrades and include most units presently occupied. Rental increases may fall in the 2% to 5% range annually, in non–24–hour cities. That's pretty straight–forward.

Rent growth is just one component of aggregate revenue but it really drives NOI. One reason is because it costs less money to retain the same resident (versus the expenses associated with turnover) than it does to capture a new resident.

Where and how do you find rent growth? In market and submarket analysis (see chapter 2). Turnover can be a good thing when rents are significantly below current market rates. Rent growth can be expanded with turnover as below market rents are raised to current market rents.

Turnover refers to the time when one resident moves out and another resident moves in. The rental property is "turned" or made ready, for the next resident. At turnover the rental property is inspected for any necessary repairs, and is painted and cleaned prior to being advertised for rent. This is the point in time where market rate rent capture is anticipated. If the rental property is made ready as a competitive product in its market, then capturing market rate rental revenue is the goal.

What is Rent Growth?

Rent growth is like compound interest: it grows from a baseline of (rental) income already in hand but requires an up–front investment. With income property there are dozens of potential income sources, from late fees to storage, valet services and dog sitting. But at the end of the day, with any income property, more than 90% of revenue comes from rents. Thus, growth in rents drives higher revenue the fastest.

Rent growth measures take into account dramatic occurrences or intentional causes that management or ownership implement on a property, allowing you to measure potential significant changes in rental income based on changes in operational occurrences. For example: Is there a big difference between current rents and potential rents if you were to perform complete remodels? If the answer is yes, then you will want to know, and measure, the return on investment prior to making this investment in redevelopment.

Consider the following cost versus benefit example: if a $10,000 investment in upgrades will generate $12,000 in annual rent growth that is a great investment. If a $50,000 investment in upgrades will garner $2,000 in annual increased rent then there is not much incentive to make the investment in upgrades. Rent growth ties directly to the rent roll. Rent growth comes from new and existing leases or from units that are vacated and upgraded to create freshness or differentiation to capture additional rent.

One method to assure lower turnover is to eliminate rental rate increases. This is a terrible business strategy, however, and will result in rental income deterioration in rapid fashion. Increasing rents will create some turnover, but along with it comes an opportunity to upgrade facilities and charge higher rents for these upgrades.

Consider the bigger the gap between current rents and Gross Potential Rent, the greater the incentive to upgrade interior space to capture this additional rent and close the gap between current rents and GPR.

In many of the following metrics, you are converting rent growth results to a monthly number. Why? Because rents are collected monthly and because bills, including mortgage payments, are paid monthly. Because your banker doesn't care what your annual income is if you cannot meet your next monthly mortgage payment. And because you can always multiply by twelve to obtain annual figures.

Following are metrics you can create, pre–appraisal, from your rent roll numbers. These same metrics can be created for competitive properties as well. These metrics have significant value for analysis when there are multiple years of data. With only a single year of financials to review, this data requires further delineation into monthly and quarterly values to view the direction of trends. Note that in this chapter, you are measuring <u>rent</u> and not revenue. All of these measures set up the ability to create trendlines.

Rent per square foot (gross)

Gross square footage includes all rentable space and all common area under roof. Common area includes interior hallways, clubhouse and office space. For an office property, this will include built public space and perhaps a leasing office, maintenance and storage space in use for the upkeep of the property. This is an important measure because it brings into view the cost of operations for the entire asset versus the cost of maintaining leased space.

The formula: Most recent 12–months collected rents (per the rent roll) divided by total square feet under roof (excluding garages and below grade storage), divided by 12 months. This number is referred to as an amount of rent per square foot (gross) per month.

Example: A 154–unit multifamily building of one and two bedroom apartments has annual rental revenue of $1.20M. The property has interior hallways, an office and a clubhouse. Rentable square feet is 125,000 and total square feet under roof is 133,000. Rent per square foot (gross) is .75 cents per square foot per month.

$$\text{Rent per square foot (gross):} \quad = \quad \frac{\$\,1.20M}{133{,}000 \text{ sq. ft.}} \quad = \quad \$9.02$$

$$= \quad \frac{\$9.02}{12 \text{ months}} \quad = \quad \$\,0.75$$

Rent per square foot (net rentable)

Rent per square foot utilizes rent only as the numerator—and no other revenue. Rent per square foot (net rentable) refers to livable, rentable space, or interior living space.

The formula: Total annual rent divided by the total number of rentable square feet, divided by 12. Multiply this number by twelve to obtain the annual rent per square foot.

Example: Rent of $489,600 divided by 48,000 rentable sq ft = $10.20 rent per square foot per year, divided by 12 months =.85 cents per month.

$$\text{Rent per Square Foot (net):} \quad = \quad \frac{\$489,600}{48,000 \text{ sq. ft.}} \quad = \quad \$10.20$$

$$= \quad \frac{\$\ 10.20}{12 \text{ Months}} \quad = \quad \$\ 0.85$$

Annual rent per unit

The constant in this formula is the number of units, occupied or not. The number of units is the total number of units in the development.

The formula: Total annual collected rent divided by total number of units.

Example: For a 144 unit building annual collected rent is $1,719,000. Annual rent per unit is $11,937 or $995 per unit per month.

$$\text{Annual rent per unit} \quad = \quad \frac{\$1,719,000}{144 \text{ units}} \quad = \quad \$11,937$$

$$= \quad \frac{\$11,937}{12 \text{ Months}} \quad = \quad \$995$$

This number represents "collected" rents, not Gross Potential Rent (GPR) or Stated Lease Rent (SLR). You are measuring collected rent generated per unit per year.

Annual rent per occupied unit

Rent per occupied unit is constructed from average annual occupancy. If the average occupancy for a 100–unit development is 90%, then for a multifamily asset presume 90 units occupied over the course of the last year.

The formula: Total annual rent divided by the average number of occupied units.

Example: 144 units has averaged 93% occupancy during the last 12–months. Rental revenue for this period was $1,719,000. We have 144 units multiplied by 93% occupancy = 134 occupied units. Dividing annual rental revenue of $1,719,000 by 134 units equates to annual rent per occupied unit of $12,828 per unit per year or $1,069 per occupied unit per month.

$$\text{Annual rent per occupied unit} = \frac{\$1,719,000}{134 \text{ units}} = \$12,828$$

$$= \frac{\$12,828}{12 \text{ Months}} = \$1,069$$

These last two data points demonstrate that occupied units create greater revenue. The value here is the creation of measures that allow for tracking trends in rent growth for a rental property asset. Having access to two years of rental history (or three years if possible) will generate a trendline allowing you to measure rent per unit and rent growth per unit.

Having monthly rental revenue numbers and a simple spreadsheet you can chart changes in rent comparing these two data points: annual rent per unit as compared to annual rent per occupied unit. This disparity between the two numbers allows you to capture vacancy loss in real dollars. Knowing this number allows for creating a plan of action to reduce vacancy losses.

Average length of tenancy

Imagine having a crystal ball prior to making an acquisition. If you could know any one thing about the property, what would you want to know? My one provocative question: What is the average length of tenancy? This is best determined in months. For income–producing properties, one of the greatest cash eaters is turnover. This is why resident screening is so very important. Determining average length of tenancy is a necessary step to understanding strength of income for an income–producing asset.

Identifying average length of tenancy is a significant determinant of resident stability.

You want a quality resident base that represents a good fit for the asset and one you hope to retain for a long time. Consistently high turnover based on poor tenant credit quality can erode gains in rent growth, in addition to creating costs that exceed security deposits. For multifamily income property, the average turnover rate nationally is 50 percent per year. This means that for every 100 units rented, 50 tenants will move out at the end of the initial lease term.

The formula: From the rent roll, for each occupied unit, determine the month of move–in and count the total number of months each resident has occupied their unit. Represent each unit in months occupied. Total this number and divide it by the total number of occupied units.

Example: A 24 unit building presently has 21 occupied units. Seven tenants have lived there for 11 months, seven for 12 months and 7 for 13 months. (7x11) + (7x12) + (7x13) = 252 total months. Divide this number by 21 (the total number of occupied units) and the average length of tenancy is 12 months; 252 months divided by 21 units = 12 months.

$$\text{Average length of tenancy} = \frac{252 \text{ months}}{21 \text{ units}} = 12 \text{ Months}$$

Extended average length of tenancy can be a positive or negative. If the rental rate of occupied units is keeping pace with market rents the results can be fantastic as revenue increases without a corresponding increase in turnover costs. On the other hand, if rents in occupied units are stagnant or collections issues prevail, then while length of tenancy is longer, revenue actually suffers. To presume that length of tenancy in and of itself is the sole determining factor in rent stability is incorrect.

Rent growth is captured by pacing rental increase with Gross Potential Rent and the application of appropriate property upgrades to position an asset to compete at market rental rates. By tracking rent per square foot, and the other measures presented in this chapter, you can identify vacancy loss and opportunities to move rents towards market rates.

Chapter 5:
Revenue Growth
Metrics

Revenue encompasses all sources of income from an income–producing asset: rents, late fees, parking, garage and storage rent, soap sales (from the laundry area), every source of income is listed under revenue. These metrics go beyond rental income generation and encompass all revenue sources.

You determine revenue growth from a review of historic financials. What is the increase in revenue year–over–year, first, for the rent roll in its entirety; next, for each individual unit. Why this? To identify if revenue is increasing from rental rate increases or through some other means.

Revenue growth relies heavily on the ability to raise rents to market rates. Length of tenancy is a factor. There is a correlation between rental increases and turnover. Excluding a discussion on rent control, a tenant base with years of occupancy will generate lower rents than a tenant base with normal turnover rates (remember, for multifamily properties the average turnover is 50% per year). The reason is because average year–over–year rental increases are, generally speaking, less than what a dynamic market will generate.

A property manager works hard to maintain a consistently high level of occupancy. Attempting to raise every rent to market rate every year can create a significant increase in turnover, thus creating high turnover costs. The by–product of this can be less revenue. It is a constant balancing act.

Having historic and current revenue figures for a set period of time you can calculate percentage change. You are looking for year–over–year changes or month–over–month measuring the same month from one year prior. You can also see trends based on comparing year–over–year quarterly data which takes into account seasonal differences.

When you compare revenue per unit year–over–year consider this as similar to the "same store sales" metric used in retail and restaurants. Each of the following metrics allows us to measure this percentage change in revenue.

Revenue per square foot (gross)

Revenue per square foot is the most recent 12–month revenue divided by total square feet under roof. This includes interior hallways and common areas, but not garages.

Example: $300,000 in annual revenue divided by a development with 26,000 total square feet. The result equates to revenue per square foot. In this example, that number is $11.54 per square foot per year, or .96 cents per square foot per month.

$$\text{Revenue per square foot (gross)} = \frac{\$300,000}{26,000 \text{ sq. ft.}} = \$11.54$$

$$= \frac{\$11.54}{12 \text{ Months}} = \$0.96$$

Revenue per square foot (rentable)

Most recent 12–months revenue (per the rent roll) divided by total rentable square feet. Rentable square feet is livable space that is or can be rented; space that is or will produce revenue.

Example: $500,000 in annual revenue divided by a development with 42,000 rentable square feet. The result equates to revenue per rentable square feet of $11.90 annually or .99 cents per rentable square foot per month, or per unit per year.

$$\text{Revenue per square foot (rentable)} = \frac{\$500,000}{42,000 \text{ sq. ft.}} = \$11.90$$

$$= \frac{\$11.90}{12 \text{ Months}} = \$0.99$$

Annual revenue per unit

This is a multifamily apartment formula or for someone with a portfolio of single–family rentals. The constant in this formula is the number of units. Whether occupied or not, the number of units remains the same. Take annual revenue and divide this by the total number of units.

Example: The property is 84 units with annual revenue of $954,000 (rents and all other revenue). Revenue per unit is $11,357 per unit per year.

$$\text{Annual revenue per unit} \quad = \quad \frac{\$954,000}{84 \text{ units}} \quad = \quad \$11,357$$

$$= \quad \frac{\$11,357}{12 \text{ Months}} \quad = \quad \$946$$

Annual revenue per occupied unit

Revenue per occupied unit is calculated using total annual revenue and average annual occupancy. Divide total revenue by the average number of occupied units.

Example: If the average occupancy for a 100–unit development is 90%, then presume 90 units occupied over the course of the year. If annual revenue is $795,000 then annual revenue per unit is $8,833 per unit per year. $795,000 divided by 90 units = $8,833 per occupied unit per year.

$$\text{Annual Revenue per Occupied Unit} \quad = \quad \frac{\$795,000}{90 \text{ units}} \quad = \quad \$8,833$$

$$= \quad \frac{\$8,833}{12 \text{ Months}} \quad = \quad \$736$$

Revenue – Ancillary Income

The category ancillary income is any collected income not classified as rental income. While secondary to the big money (rents), ancillary income represents a stream of revenue that compliments rents and often represents pure cash flow after expenses. As with a burger joint, sometimes the profit is in the pickle.

Is there a way to juice the revenue side of rental property without raising rents? Absolutely. It's called ancillary income. Property management is charged with implementing this from a solutions perspective as most non–rental income provides a service to your residents.

The vast majority of revenue from rental property operations is derived from rental revenue. Great, good, wonderful; how boring is that? Actually, it's wonderfully boring in a stabilized asset, particularly if you can keep turnover down. On top of rent there are an increasing number of potential income sources related to property ownership. We discuss them here as ancillary income.

The lease is the controlling document for the vast majority of income (rental income). The lease can generate access to other income sources. Think of ancillary income as a menu of services for your residents. Some will be imposed for not adhering to the terms of the lease (example: late fees) while others are completely optional (example: covered parking).

Many high yielding multifamily investment properties will have high levels of other income. There's a reason for this. Sometimes high ancillary income is a testament to the property manager or ownership group. They are just that good and diligent about enforcing the rights afforded the Landlord via the terms of the lease. In some instances, ancillary income is all late fees. Consistently high late fees, while looking good on the income statement, are a testament to the credit quality of the tenant base. And you can bet management is working overtime in collections.

When a rental property is for sale, ancillary income can show big numbers when an owner/seller is looking to bolster their profit/loss statement presenting high numbers to a potential buyer. Good business? No. Happens all the time? Yes. Just like with rents, you need validation of these income sources.

Beyond rental revenue, what other opportunities for revenue growth can we identify? Following is a list offering a good place to start.

Appliances. Do you rent appliances? Is this a good idea? Washer and dryer sets are the most requested. First, the unit must have an area for the appliance that meets local building codes. If it is necessary to "rig" the set up, then please, do not install anything. Assuming there are appropriate washer and dryer hookups (including for exhaust), then the value proposition is this: If the install results in the rental of one or two additional units and the costs of the actual appliances have a one or two year payback, then the action is additive to revenue. This is because without the appliances there are two more vacant units than there would have been otherwise.

Application fees. The application fee is usually a wash as the fee collected offsets the direct costs of obtaining credit information and completing employment verification. Application fees can be used as a "screen out" function or a concession. When struggling to get people in the door this fee can be waived removing a barrier to entry.

Break—up fees. A break—up fee is paid when a lease is broken. Rather than have a resident pay for the remaining lease term (which is often improbable), the breakup fee may be one month's rent and forfeiture of security deposit.

Late fees. Late fees in C—class multifamily properties can represent as much as ten percent of revenue. A C—class property is usually older, in a less desirable part of town and in desperate need of updates. Of course, collecting late fees requires increased time, energy and effort. As part of the lease, late fees must be enforced fairly and evenly. It is imperative not to play games or show favoritism both from a legal and financial perspective.

Pet fees. If your rental property allows pets, then income from pet fees is required to offset the added costs associated with having pets on property. Like application fees, this is not a money maker but an offset to incurred costs. And there will be costs. Limit the number and size of pets per dwelling to not more than two pets with no pet being more than 35 pounds (although charging by the pound is probably a bad idea). Also, consider making a list of prohibitive dogs based on their demeanor and representative danger to the general public.

Laundry income. This can be a major source of revenue sometimes representing as much as three to five percent of revenue. The industry has evolved to the point where there are divisions within commercial laundry companies that specialize in the operation and maintenance of laundry facilities on multifamily developments.

Internet and cable. Some cable operators offer a percentage over–ride for delivering customers to their service. This can range from 2–10% of cable revenue. Every market is unique depending on the local competition. Ask about anticipated apartment–wide product penetration and if there are minimum monthly fees payable to the service provider per unit (occupied or not). This industry, as it relates to apartments, is bigger than laundry services. Shop around and compare service providers. There is an array of services, some simple, and some very complex. Take your time implementing this because contractual terms can be five and ten years.

Parking. Parking is a microcosm of economics where scarcity leads to higher prices. In many urban areas parking is no longer a right but a privilege. As the housing stock has aged, the ratio of parking spaces to units has decreased significantly. Apartment buildings built in the 1950's and 60's presumed one car and one bread winner per household. In the 1970's many cars were bigger than a standard parking space. Present day, many two bedrooms have two roommates. And they each have their own car. Fees are market specific and may include the following:

- Off street, single space parking

- Covered parking

- Garage parking

On site storage. The storage industry is huge in America. Being able to offer storage at an apartment community is a bonus not only in potential income but a quality attribute to sell to tenants and potential tenants. They can keep their "stuff" close by.

Concierge services. This can range from laundry pick up/delivery to dog walking. Many concierge services can be out–sourced so that the apartment property is obtaining a referral fee from the service provider. Stay away from certain personal services like baby–sitting and auto detailing. In both of these examples the risk/reward ratio is not aligned.

RUBS, This stands for "Renter Utility Billing System." RUBS service providers assist property owners in implementing individual metering of apartment homes that are presently on a single, central meter. This can be for water, electric or natural gas usage. Similar to laundry equipment and servicing for apartments, this is an entire industry with many service providers to choose from. There is no single market leader.

Non–refundable deposits Note: this does not say "security deposit" fees. Different states treat this in varying ways. In some instances you may charge a non–refundable fee in lieu of a security deposit. The risk is if the resident causes significantly more damage than is covered by the 'fee' then there is no potential recovery. Some companies are testing this as an annual fee and ear–marking funds for capital expenditures or general upkeep.

Insurance fees Having the ability to write, sell or earn fees on insurance products requires state–issued licensing. With larger properties the value add is worthwhile. Some property owners require all tenants to carry renters insurance. Granted, they cannot tell tenants where to purchase said insurance, but they do make referrals to providers. Appropriate licensing is key.

Security deposit forfeitures Security deposit forfeiture income occurs when a unit is abandoned, but this varies by state, as does the definition of causes for forfeiture.

As you can see, for rental property owners there are many alternative income sources to pursue in addition to rental income. Start with the ideas you believe will be most utilized by your residents and expand accordingly.

Consider the ancillary income line items presented here as a starter list. The category will continue to expand. Depending on the property and income level of residents, sources may expand to include in–home massages and manicures, teeth whitening, interior designers, chefs, solar on roofs, move–in fees, cell towers, green space…the list will gain length and complexity over time.

Chapter 6:
Documenting Revenue

Rent roll analysis joins discovery and baseline data to present a detailed financial snapshot of a rental property. Collectively, discovery and baseline data present a compelling case to either proceed with a rental property acquisition or a step away. Assume for a moment that the only information you may obtain about a potential acquisition candidate is from what is presented in this chapter. If that was in fact true, you would likely have a solid opinion of the asset at the conclusion of your review.

Discovery

Discovery is a form of gathering information, usually related to a legal proceeding or lawsuit. For our purposes, discovery is the gathering of information to make an informed decision related to a potential real property acquisition.

(Discovery is)... A category of procedural devices employed by a party to a civil or criminal action, prior to trial, to require the adverse party to disclose information that is essential for the preparation of the requesting party's case and that the other party alone knows or possesses. (http://legal–dictionary. thefreedictionary.com/discovery)

With respect to acquiring a property from a seller, although they are not an "adverse party" they are on the other side of the transaction. As a potential buyer of their real estate asset, you are compelled to request information that the seller alone "knows or possesses."

A match point in tennis is any point that will end the contest with victory assigned to the winner. In singles tennis there is only one winner. In a real estate acquisition, match point is the conclusion of an asset transfer from a willing buyer to a willing seller where both parties are able to meet their objectives (their overall objective, not every single objective). With a well–conceived real estate transaction, both buyer and seller can win.

What can assist in getting to match point better than anything else is agreement on the income derived from the real estate asset; to whit, belief in the validity of the rent roll. The best case scenario for this to occur is that income reflected on the rent roll matches perfectly with contractual income presented from executed, in–force leases. All points lead back to the numbers on the rent roll with relevant dates.

Numbers on the Rent Roll – Date Certain

Projected lease rent and collected rent seldom equal in any given month for various reasons: slow pay tenants, a change in lease terms not reflected on the rent roll, unscheduled move–outs, a new lease. You always want your numbers to "tie out." In accounting speak, this simply means you want to be able to trace (or vouch for) the paper trail that led to the conclusions reached about a given number. You want to see that utilities paid match utility bills; that pet fees tie to pets on property; and that rental income ties to in–place leases.

You will begin to gain agreement on rent roll numbers by attaining a "date certain" (or selected date range) concurrence with the seller. In all likelihood the parties agree on more than 90% of the numbers presented. It's that pesky ten percent that keeps rent revenue from becoming a static number. The workaround is for the parties to agree that rental revenue is X dollars as of a specified date. Argue all you want around other dates, but with both buyer and seller agreeing on rental revenue even for the briefest of times (a given month, quarter or year) the probability of reaching a closing date increases exponentially. Why? Because once the date or date range is agreed to, you are exclusively reviewing rental revenue numbers for that time frame and no other. Deep in the Realpage.com website is the explanation for a report entitled, "Rent Roll Detail." Following is the first sentence explaining the outputs of this report.

"The Rent Roll Detail report is a comprehensive snapshot of the units at your property as of a specified date."

The analysis requires a self–generated synopsis of the rent roll taken straight from leases. It sounds so simple. Like an Olympic sprinter, the idea is to cover the same exact distance as every other runner in the race...except with a little more exacting technique, striding a little more precisely than anyone else. Attorneys refer to this as a lease abstract. But we are not attorneys; we are buyers, sellers and operators of rental property. What we are "extracting" from the lease is just the information necessary to create an accurate rent roll.

In large commercial transactions (non–residential) buyers will require estoppels from each tenant validating the rents, terms and timing of each lease. An estoppel is a document signed by the tenant that affirms certain information in the lease document, primarily the terms, payments and expiration of the lease term.

Your rent roll will include Gross Potential Rent (GPR) as a marker, stated rent (from in–force leases) and collected rent (rent received or actually collected where a bank statement may substitute). It is very seldom that all three numbers are the same. Let's assume Unit #B was rented two years ago for $750 monthly. Based on changes in the local market, that same unit could be rented today for $850. However, rental rate increases in occupied units do not always pace with market rents without purposeful management making this occur.

In this example, let's assume today's rent is $795. The owner may have attempted to keep pace with market rates or rents may be raised "just cuz" (it happens all the time). Bob wants every unit rented at $20 higher than last year; never mind a $50 annual increase is a reasonable expectation. This partly explains the disparity between GPR and actual lease rents.

Recognition of a lease extension beyond the initial lease term is validated by documentation in the lease file. This is done with a simple lease extension form. Simple as it may be, it has teeth with respect to conferring an added amount of time to the existing, in–place lease. Place the revised end date of the lease on the rent roll. These dates are important and have use beyond just knowing when leases expire.

They can provide average length of tenancy, for example, and assist in creating a plan for lease renewals.

Baseline Data

Baseline data is fact–based information used in the creation of the rent roll. Baseline data is everything collected to insert into the rent roll with the objective of validating rental income. Baseline data includes property and financial information provided from sources other than the seller or seller's representative. It includes your review of the leases, your research, information from public records and third–party sources. Your collection of baseline data includes:

- Gross Potential Rent (GPR)

- Income

- Expenses

- Vacancy

- Address

- Unit Numbers

- Built Square Feet

Gross Potential Rent (GPR) comes from due diligence, local contacts and a review of market rates advertised by competitive properties. The next three items can be identified from public record sources. Note: an old appraisal is not a public record, no matter the source of the appraisal. Where did the appraiser get their information? Who knows? Independent validation is your best friend here.

Baseline data is basic information gathered by your team. It is used later to provide a comparison for assessing facts provided by ownership or management.

Gross Potential Rents (GPR) is a constant part of the equation. The GPR number is a reflection of maximizing rents on a daily basis. GPR is a present day representation of current market rents. It is always changing based on market dynamics. When a newly–constructed property enters the market, competitive properties will adapt by changing tactics and rental pricing in an attempt to compete favorably with the newest competition.

Baseline Income. A review of the rent roll requires two sets of data: one for the most recent full month and one for the same month from the previous year (two years if you can get it). The objective is to establish a baseline to determine current income and having as a comparison a recent historic reflection for the same period from the previous year.

One of the first items to review on the two rent rolls (the most recent full month versus one year prior) is to note if there are unit numbers that have remained vacant during both periods. If yes, the rationalization may be normalized turnover. This can be validated during the 100% walk–through during the due diligence period.

However, since presumption is the mother of all assumptions, unless and until it is validated that units 100, 102, 103 and 104 (and eight others) were all vacant during both periods on the rent roll due to normalized turnover, presume these units to be "off line." Off line means that you must presume these units were non–income generating for the entire twelve–month period. The question to ask is why they were off line. Sometimes the answer is obvious, other times it is hidden in the walls. The physical inspection process performed by professionals will usually provide answers to the non–obvious.

There are worst case scenarios to consider. Such as a prior resident who is a professional drywall installer. He was very upset about his pending eviction. So he cut large holes in the wall of his unit and dumped fish into the walls… lots of fish. Then, he repaired the drywall and painted the wall fresh as he left the building. In a few days the entire building smelled of…something. So much so that everyone had to move out of the building. The point is, if a particular rental unit or building is vacant, find out why with a high degree of certainty.

Baseline Expenses. Similar in every way to baseline income, baseline expenses are those expenses that you can verify independently. The easiest one is the real estate tax bill, which is almost always a matter of public record. Others include utility bills and insurance costs.

Without having direct bills from management or ownership, gaining access to this information requires contacting local service providers and finding out what you can without being intrusive. It's one thing to have copies of bills, quite another to cold call Electric Company of Ohio and ask what property 123 Main Street spent on electric last year. It can be important as some units rented could be with "all bills paid" by the owner. You are looking for independent verification on actual bills paid.

Baseline Vacancy. The most expensive space at any rental property is empty space. A vacant space is space available for lease that is not leased. A rental property is a perishable commodity. When a cruise ship leaves port for the week, vacancy is set in stone for the entire cruise. In rental property, there is a stationary asset but still multiple "cabins." Every day of vacancy is a day of lost revenue that cannot be recouped. How many units were vacant in the most recent 12–month period? Convert units vacant into days/months. It's amazing how much of an impact this number can have. The opportunity cost here is measurable and you can measure lost revenue tied to long–term vacancy.

The obvious cause of extended vacancy, if there are huge issues all around, is usually staring us in the face when walking the property: current ownership or current management. Do they seem competent? Is there financial distress? When performing magic tricks and investing in income property make sure to not fool yourself. Do not let sympathy or a distressed situation color your investment decision judgment. When buying rental property there are no short–cuts. Find out the reason for the vacancy.

Let's get the address. On numerous occasions through the years I have identified a property address completely different than the one received from the broker, site manager or owner. Sometimes it's a simple error, other times a very significant factor, when for example, an adjacent vacant lot is represented as part of the property when in fact it belongs to the same owner but is not being offered with the for sale asset. Is this an omission or just an oversight? Either way, it is up to you to know the address and what property precisely is represented by an address.

Unit numbers. This may seem tedious, but stick with it here. Have you ever seen a four–plex with a fifth unit in the basement? How many units are there? From my perspective there are only four unless that fifth unit has a publicly acknowledged address (and probably its own electric meter). If the seller is representing the building as a five–plex but only four units are of public record (i.e., existing on tax rolls, etc.), then there are only four units.

In big cities it is not uncommon for families to live in garages behind the house. Sure, this may represent rental income, but do you really want to consider that as stable, forward–looking income? Probably not. Count unit numbers from public records only. Then count doors. See if this matches up with the information provided you by the seller. Then count utility meters. The expected conclusion of this exercise is the number of utility meters equals the number of units. There could be one additional meter per building based on common area lighting or laundry facilities.

Built square feet under roof. Remember the discussion of gross square feet versus rentable square feet? It's odd that so many people can measure the same exact space and come up with varying numbers. It's like counting pieces of pepperoni on pizzas—there is never the same number. When attempting to determine built square feet from public records, the information is often limited, particularly if the property is more than 20 years old. Some assessor's offices keep detailed records including built square feet; others have nothing on the matter.

Budgets – Historic and Projected

Your documented revenue is the starting point for creating the post–closing budget. Do you have an operating budget for your newly acquired, or soon to be acquired, real estate asset? Too many new owners never think about hiring management until the day after closing—like the property is going to manage itself for a month or so. Not! The same applies to having a budget; it can't wait until day one comes.

If you have performed the appropriate due diligence then you have relevant historic budgets in your possession. Pre–acquisition, the next course of action is creating a budget for the first full year of operations and sketching out a projected budget going forward at least 12–months past the first full 12–months of operations.

The over–simplified budgeting process is accomplished by reviewing last year's budget and comparing it with actual results. Then, the reviewer splits (between last years' budget and actual results) after adding a few percentage points to revenue and expense categories. No! Budgeting must be a "value add" proposition.

Annual budgeting must take into account the realities of each asset: the financial, physical and local market competitiveness. A picture perfect asset with 300 newly–built units across the street in a market with slow absorption has to factor in the impact of competition. These factors affect the budget and viability of the asset.

Static number crunching that entails moving last year's actuals into next year's column precludes original thought or reality. The originality necessary in this process is taking current market dynamics into consideration during the budgeting process. This view may require utilizing additional facets of your existing suites software or redeploying marketing savings into resident premiums to maintain resident retention. Or perhaps taking savings from utility usage reductions and deploying these dollars into management staff training with measurable results.

When the annual budgeting process is considered more than a perfunctory number crunching exercise, positive outputs can prevail. There is more to budgeting than making assumptions and passing them up the food chain. Thinking of budgeting as a "value add" process makes the entire endeavor much more exciting and potentially profitable.

Bank Statements

Having the ability to review just a few months' bank statements adds a great deal of credibility to the seller's presented numbers. A happy day is when a review finds rent roll collections balance precisely with receipts as reflected in the monthly bank statements, month in, and month out. Sellers are sometimes hesitant to provide bank statements ("hesitant" is an understatement). This hesitation is not necessarily for reasons you may think. For some owners, "opening the books" is the first ever entry point of having complete strangers review their financial dealings. The level of discomfort is inversely related to the size of the asset; smaller property owners will have a higher degree of hesitation. Why?

Unfortunately, many owners and operators of small income properties under–report rental income. This is never a good idea on so many levels, from issues with the IRS to the discussion we are having throughout this book on validating rental income. When it comes time to sell an asset, credibility drops like a rock in still water when a seller says they have two sets of books, or represents that income is higher than the rent roll suggests because of_____ (fill in the blank here). As they say, "Life is too short" for phony numbers. Yes, we can re–construct actual operations if necessary. But if you suspect fraud or misrepresentation, unless the deal in question has some serious upside potential or represents a strategic value to your portfolio, why bother with the commitment required for rent roll analysis? My advice... move on.

Bank statements are bedrock. Bank statements provide quantitative perfection and an ironclad transactional record. There is no better source of the truth...if they are true original bank statements. Thievery and lying have been around since the dawn of man. People are just better and faster at it now. Case in point: Advances in printing technology keeps the Department of the Treasury hopping to assure our currency remains near impossible to forge. But this only makes certain criminals try harder.

For starters, if you are fortunate enough to obtain bank statements, call the bank in question to see if the account is real. This is a no–cost, easy task to accomplish. The biggest threat to the validity of bank statements is cash. Has a seller added cash to deposits to make income higher? Is a seller using cash to pay for expenses so they are hidden, thus making recorded expenses smaller?

At the end of the day, understating income is reflected in an undervaluation of the asset.

The premise for this statement is that if income is not verifiable then it does not exist. Here comes the "yes buts'" from sellers. "We never deposit laundry income" or, "Some tenants always pay in cash so we just pocket that." Now that's a problem. You are looking at the purchase of a hard asset based on verifiable income and expenses. Without verification, it cannot be counted. Such representations also bring into question the validity of any and all other information presented by the seller because if income is misrepresented then it is only natural to wonder what other areas fall into the same gray.

The question will arise about "which" bank statements? The bank statements you want to see are for the accounts that receive rental receipts and those used to pay expenses. These can be different statements from different banks. You want to review statements for each active account.

Sometimes you will hear much murmuring with this request for bank statements. Be reasonable, make it a doable thing, but convey its necessity to tie off your due diligence. When buying a long–term asset..."It's your money." This is no time to be shy about acquiring facts and figures.

As a potential buyer of an income property, you need validation of income. "Stories" are of limited assistance in this pursuit. You need those bank statements. This may seem harsh but consider them as a required part of the documentation path that allows for a picture-perfect correlation between one months' collected income and expenses.

Let's say the numbers seem to be...bouncy. They're just not adding up. The fastest way to see clearly is to review bank statements. You are looking for deposits on the bank statement to correlate quickly with receipts. If not, why not?

With larger commercial assets, many of the individuals involved have been to the rodeo before, where "the list" of requested documents may be in a different order than the last deal the items on the list are the same: bank statements, two years' financials, tax returns, etc. Obstinacy or slowness with the professionals usually has more to do with workload than hesitation to comply. At the asset management level no bank statements are available as they are not involved in the day–to–day operations.

Tax Returns

Will the seller provide tax returns? One of the things we have attempted to avoid in this book is to pigeonhole the size of the deal or to formulate presumption like, "the bigger the deal size the less analysis required." There is no guarantee that as a buyer of income property the sellers will provide you with tax returns. You can get huffy, mad or indignant and say, "Well then, the deal is off." Fine, you just killed half your deal flow.

Is there really such a thing as an "original" tax return anymore? More people e–file than ever before and who do you call to confirm that the tax returns delivered to you are those actually filed by the seller? There are no easy answers, but here are some guidelines.

- Request tax returns along with all the other documentation and see if the tax returns show up. If yes, great. If no, then request them again at the same time as the request for additional information.

- Ask the seller for permission to contact their accountant for property tax returns. This takes the onus off the seller to go get stuff and the accountant is a reliable third–party source for this very important information.

- Once you have the tax returns in hand, review first for completeness, page count and consistency. Are all pages done by hand or electronic? Are there pages missing? Are the return(s) presented for the most recent year(s)?

It is good to have tax returns as another checkpoint to cross reference represented income and expenses. But they are not absolutely necessary to get the deal done. Bank statements are far more important as they assist in tracking income and expenses for due diligence. Never turn down tax returns, but consider them as just one more layer in building the case for represented income and expenses, not the only layer.

Documenting the documents can directly impact your comfort level with a property. They represent various parts of the puzzle. The easier they come together the higher your level of confidence in your ultimate buy or no buy decision. This is the benefit of having superior financial information from your own due diligence.

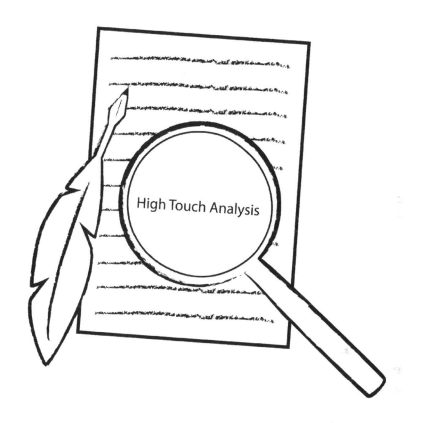

Chapter 7:
High–touch Analysis

In marketing, the term high–touch refers to actual interaction between either a company's products or personnel and the end user of their products. For our purposes here, high–touch refers to the ability of the buyer or buyer's representative to review original documents <u>in person</u> and perform an on–site visit to further authenticate the validity of financial information presented by the seller.

A simple but powerful example of the power of "originals" is the story of a borrower who e–mailed a PDF of a letter to the lender stating his associates were "now willing" to proceed with the equity discussed in prior correspondence in support of a new loan. The banker proceeded with the loan based on these assurances only to find out that the *original* letter stated that the associates were "not willing" to proceed. What a difference a letter can make!

Lease File Review– The heart of the matter

Leases are the bedrock of contractual rental revenue. As a potential owner of a particular income–producing asset, my preferred first response to agreement on price is "Show me the leases." Leases are the link to the dollars; they are the critical element in the paper trail to the pot of gold. I have personally reviewed thousands of lease files. It's boring, it's monotonous, it's necessary. It is the absolute heart of the matter when it comes to understanding the credit quality of the income stream from an income–producing real property asset.

In modern times on many commercial leases the actual street address of leased premises is all too often absent. The lease is between ABC, LLC and XYZ Corporation, for example. Leases in use are also vague in many instances. Authority to grant a lease can be represented by a management company, sometimes by the named property (with or without legal standing) and other times by the actual owner. Confusion reigns!

During the lease file review do not collect credit scores! This is proprietary information provided by the resident to the current owner or manager. As a potential buyer you are not a party to the contract lease and have no right to obtain this information. You may note the general tendency of credit scores, in aggregate, but you may not collect individual credit scores.

A lease can be a simple matter. The objective of a lease is to set out the terms and conditions under which one party grants use of certain premises to another party for a certain length of time, for a certain amount of money.

The lease file review is a critical part of determining the validity of contractual rental income as presented on the rent roll.

A lease abstract is a summary of the key information points within the lease. A simple lease file abstract on a single spreadsheet allows for collection of the pertinent information you are looking for to validate the rent roll. Here is a list of items to review from each lease file:

- Original lease with original signature(s)

- Amount of current contractual rent

- Lease start date and original lease end date

- Latest lease renewal, signed (prefer all prior renewals in order, latest one on top)

- Original application with signature(s)

- Confirmation of credit check

- Confirmation of criminal background check

The first order of business when performing a lease file review is to make sure the party granting the lease has the authority to do so. Consider a lease as a binding contract and it all makes sense: You want to know if the signing authority can bind the agreement.

Then verify if the lease is valid and in–force. Sounds simple, right? However, too many owners/managers get lazy and fail to renew expired leases in writing. It's a simple process in many instances, but too often left undone. Renewals are crucial to validating credible future income. Renewals provide an opportunity to move rents forward (read: increase rents). The lease designates the timing for this event and the lease renewal creates an opportune time for this event to occur.

Next question: are all leases 12–month leases? Stabilized income property is presumed to have 12–month leases. You are here to validate the rent roll so you must know the lease terms. Presumption is not an option. Your analysis generates an output for each individual lease with a lease start date and a lease end date. Beyond the initial lease term you want to see documentation that extends the lease for the next period of time (preferably a year). The lease renewal or lease extension document is a reflection of the in–place resident making a commitment to remain a resident for another year. No commitment, no future income, right?

Too many leases are in effect for one year and then roll into a "month–to–month." This is a very weak document and harms the value of the asset. Granted, there is occasional cause for implementing month–to–month leases, but on behalf of the property owner (or buyer) you want to see annualized leases. This extends the income stream and provides comfort to a potential buyer that a mass exodus (for any given reason) is less likely. Having leases with valid annual lease extensions in place strengthens rental income.

If a high percentage of leases have expired, then the underlying value of the income is weakened. As the new owner/manager one of your first tasks will be to renew any and all expired leases. Presume for a moment that during this process a significant number of tenants decide to move out all at once. Frankly, you have no recourse as there is no valid lease extension in place.

Noting the differential between in–place rents and current market rates, as determined by Gross Potential Rents (GPR), you may decide to leave any expired lease(s) "as is" through closing and raise rents post–closing. While this opens up a certain category of risk, it allows you (the new owner) complete control over each expired lease. The good news is with this level of deep rent roll analysis occurring during the due diligence phase; you can plan your course of action and have it ready to implement on "day one" of ownership.

With month–to–month leases, once you own the asset, based on the credit quality and payment history of certain tenants, you may decide to send a letter of non–renewal and start over with tenants selected by your team. Wholesale rental rate increases may cause a mass exodus. If that is the objective (empty the units, rehabilitate and raise rents to market level), then fine.

Most new owners find it easiest to settle in with their new acquisition versus vacating the place for rehabilitation and re–marketing. In my view, this settling in period is a waste of time. Have a plan of action and get to it. Cash flow waits for no one and it NEVER just happens. A proactive management stance is imperative to any form of significant success in rental property ownership.

The Site Visit

A discussion about what to do during a site visit could take up an entire book by itself. We are purposely avoiding the use of a "checklist" here. I want you to think about what you see versus running through an organized list. Consider structuring your takeaway from the site visit as a narrative, and write from sensory information rather than plain fact–based data.

As it relates to the rent roll consider the following: Does what you see on site concur with what you see on paper? This suggests a focus on subjective information, requiring a judgment call. Does what you see in person make a connection between the revenue stream and the asset? Yes, you are looking at property condition, but also "rent–ability" and sustainability. Remembering that a monthly rent roll is a single snapshot of financial occurrences, what does your on–site photo shoot say? Do the two compare? Do they concur?

To begin, if you are purchasing an asset in a market that is new or unfamiliar, you must remove your personal regional experiences and concentrate on the task at hand. West Coast people are unfamiliar with boilers and basements. East Coast people have seldom seen stucco and decorative rock landscaping. Living in any 24–hour city can make one far removed from how most of Americana actually lives (from Little Rock to Gary, Indiana…it's just not the same). Checking your biases at the start of a site visit goes a long way to viewing the subject asset properly. Architecturally and operationally, there are few simple comparable traits between 50 year old walk–ups in San Francisco and a 15 year old garden property in Birmingham, Alabama.

However, the aforementioned subjective review by no means removes the need for a checklist–based site visit that includes a thorough accounting of structural and environmental components. My objective here is to suggest that the rent roll site visit is a separate and distinct element requiring its own block of critical thinking time.

Unit Inspections

An opinion on construction quality is best quantified by architects, general contractors and structural engineers. Having professionals deliver information about the structural and mechanical integrity of a property is the best way to obtain information about functional obsolescence and remaining life.

For "real time" validation of current income, there's nothing that can replace an inspection of 100 percent of the units on property. Yes, I am suggesting that you step inside each and every unit on property and tie this on–site inspection to the rent roll (for income). This includes verifying number of bedrooms, square feet and as–built amenities. Are the units occupied? Do people really live here? This is often accomplished after validation of the numbers, but if doubt about the numbers arises early in the due diligence process, then schedule the unit inspection early in the decision–making process *prior* to devoting additional resources (read: real money) to third party reports, etc.

Are units empty for reasons of market competitiveness or ownership or management? Caveat: The low road for existing ownership is to always blame any and all operational shortcomings on management. Note that "management" resources are dictated by ownership. A shortfall of funds to repair/replace needed items doesn't automatically mean management is at fault for a lack of repairs, for example.

Current ownership, even though having cash for repairs, may limit management's access to resources. Say maintenance and maintenance supplies run 12% of revenue. Ownership enforces a policy that maintenance will not exceed ten percent of revenue. Period. Well, if true–blue maintenance is 12% then over time the property will reflect this under–spending. Is this the fault of management? Probably not. This falls to ownership.

Without getting too philosophical, under such pressure a management company will likely do all they can to retain the integrity of the asset and let the less tenant–centric maintenance remain undone., i.e. cracks in the sidewalk, common area wear and tear, extending the use of old pool furniture, etc.

Unfortunately, most unit inspections are usually saved until late in the due diligence process. Admittedly, unit inspections are time consuming, but these physical inspections allow you to cut your losses of both time and energy quickly when necessary. A random inspection of five to fifteen percent of the units starts this process. Keep records so there is no need to duplicate later when the 100% inspection is scheduled. The walk–through can validate or invalidate your collective due diligence.

There is always more to do to increase one's comfort level with the numbers. Unit inspections get the buyer beyond the pretty pictures and reports that were generated several months (maybe even six months) prior to the property being placed on the market.

Capital Needs Assessment (CNA)

Warren Buffet's Berkshire Hathaway purchased BNSF Railway recently for $26 billion. Mr. Buffet reportedly called the CEO and said, "I'm looking forward to our first century together." Indeed, Mr. Buffet knows how to plan for the future.

A Capital Needs Assessment (CNA) includes a long–term budget strategy to ensure long–term viability of a development.

A Capital Needs Assessment (CNA) can assist you in quantifying deferred maintenance and creating a timeline for disbursement of funds to remedy immediate repairs and long term capital outlays. In many instances, a CNA can tell you what not to buy. A rental property with significant deferred maintenance will require an immediate infusion of cash after purchase to make the property competitive in the market place and justify bringing market rate rents.

As the new owner of a rental property, if funds for obvious and necessary upgrades are not earmarked for immediate expenditure after purchase, then current rents (rents confirmed during due diligence) will prevail. If you have committed all available funds to the acquisition with no cash or reserves for implementing necessary upgrades identified from the CNA, then you have overpaid.

The CNA is a tool for negotiating funds for accomplishing the repairs once you own the deal. These dollars, even though negotiated in the purchase price, must be available for the repairs post–closing. This requires coordination between you and your lender to assure cash remains in the deal for addressing the deferred maintenance post–closing.

After closing, when you own the property, if capital expenditures remain deferred and routine maintenance is extended (meaning put off until later) then you have just purchased a problem child asset that will continue to deteriorate under your ownership. With smaller deals (those under $5M) you can sometimes get away with calling on local trade professionals to assess roofing, HVAC, electrical and plumbing. As the deal size increases, the necessity of a professionally prepared CNA is more critical.

A CNA can also solidify underlying value. It's good to know if a targeted investment property acquisition will need, for example, $250,000 in total repairs, and even better to know that half this number is immediate with the balance invested over a five or ten year term. Once completed, your Capital Needs Assessment is a negotiating tool, one that can create savings and profit.

Buying rental property should never be an impulse purchase. The acquisition process is a significant time commitment but one that can be very rewarding. Including a CNA in the acquisition process allows for greater confidence in your buying decision. Beyond simple maintenance, any investment of several million dollars or higher should require, as part of the buyers due diligence, an assessment of capital needs.

Think of a CNA as a physical property snapshot that captures the functional health on a particular date, similar to how an appraisal captures the estimated value of a property on a certain date. It may be the least expensive insurance you ever buy. Consider that sellers obtain insurance checks for storm damage and pocket the funds versus doing the repairs...being more than willing to sell you this same property with known but undisclosed damage.

Many owners skimp on upkeep that is historically standard operating procedure. Scheduled maintenance becomes *deferred* maintenance after a certain period of time. Routine maintenance such as changing air filters and regular pest control become optional to some owners when cash flow gets tight. As a buyer of rental property, sellers are not predisposed to share maintenance schedules. While this is not fraudulent, you should consider a lack of maintenance records of any kind to be a red flag.

A CNA points to deficiencies below the surface. A good example of a functionally failing development is the Watergate in Washington, D.C. It's been for sale for years. There are multiple small owners; a hotel, commercial office and retail space; varying lease holds and a helipad. Where do you start? It's got location. It's got name recognition. Aside from historic reputation and varying ownership, my guess is the asset also has significant deferred maintenance. It's a complex deal. Add a big capital expenditure bill to the mix and there are few buyers.

Excluding developments that were built to fail (with poor quality workmanship or materials), many properties can remain functional for many years if well maintained. Longevity and viability seldom occur accidentally. Planning, investment and proactive stewardship are required, and a CNA can prepare the asset for long–term ownership.

Fraud and Misrepresentation

Most people believe fraud identification is always the responsibility of "someone else" and they have no interest in devoting time and resources here. Yet there is a powerful reason to make this a focal point of the due diligence process. Consider the risk of discovering fraud *after* the deal has closed.

Misrepresentation of a small number, say $1,000 monthly, equates to $50,000 over five years. Misrepresentation that "all roofs are new" when in fact only eight of ten were replaced with insurance proceeds can mean $40,000 in near–term expenditures that went unaccounted for at closing.

There are occurrences in this business that are unbelievable, but real. There are bona fide incidents of people attempting to sell property they do not own or absconding with earnest money deposits. An all too common theme is inflating income or underreporting expenses to levels that represent fraudulent behavior.

How do you protect yourself? By using common sense, employing professionals and asking questions. There must be a systematic approach to performing due diligence (starting with the rent roll, of course) that allows for fraud detection.

In your quest to "document the documents," you will sometimes lose sight of tricks and traps. Here are just a few:

- The seller makes cash deposits into the property account over several months to substantiate the property is generating more income than ever.

- Off line and vacant units are represented as rented to Section 8 or subsidized tenants with the lease in the file being completely falsified.

- Tax returns presented are completely falsified.

- Expenditures for property management are manipulated to reflect "at market" or "below market" rates rather that just stating actual expense.

- Seller represents existing mortgage is assumable. After receipt of earnest money, seller presents documents about the existing loan being non–assumable and attempts to keep earnest money regardless of outcome.

- Presenting aged utility bills as reflecting current expense and usage.

- Properties used as "comps" are actually located in other, higher rent submarkets.

- Pending lawsuits are undisclosed.

These are just a few examples of the myriad landmines awaiting the unsophisticated buyer. Granted, full–time professionals can get taken as well. However, the window is narrower as people in the business full–time have a completely different frame of reference having been through the paces on multiple occasions.

Finding Fraud through Forensic Accounting

In this book we are looking for a single, simple conclusion: the truth about rental income. As throughout history, truth can be an elusive term. From before the time of Christ to today, truth has eluded those focused on obtaining it in its purest form, which is abject honesty based in fact. Enter forensic accounting.

What is forensic accounting? It is a combination of investigative skills using scientific inquiry and accounting principles to reach conclusions about the state of financial representations. Following are three solid definitions.

Forensic Accounting: a science (i.e., a department of systemized knowledge) dealing with the application of accounting facts gathered through auditing methods and procedures to resolve legal problems. Forensic accounting is much different from traditional auditing. Forensic accounting is a specialty requiring the integration of investigative, accounting, and auditing skills. The forensic accountant looks at documents and financial and other data in a critical manner in order to draw conclusions and calculate values and to identify irregular patterns and/or suspicious transactions. A forensic accountant does not merely look at the numbers but rather looks behind the numbers. Source: http://www.allbusiness.com/glossaries/forensic-accounting/4951633-1.html#ixzz1krKmRfol

Forensic accounting or financial forensics is the specialty practice area of accountancy that describes engagements that result from actual or anticipated disputes or litigation. "Forensic" means "suitable for use in a court of law", and it is to that standard and potential outcome that forensic accountants generally have to work. Source: http://en.wikipedia.org/wiki/Forensic_accounting

Forensic accounting, sometimes called investigative accounting, involves the application of accounting concepts and techniques to legal problems. Forensic accountants investigate and document financial fraud and white-collar crimes such as embezzlement. They also provide litigation support to attorneys and law enforcement agencies investigating financial wrongdoing. Source: http://legal-dictionary.thefreedictionary.com/Forensic+Accounting

What does forensic accounting have to do with buying income property? Why consider the use of forensic accounting? Think of it as another tool in the toolbox for use on an as-needed basis. Because it is a very expensive process, use of forensic accounting is "of consideration" rather than standard operating procedure for acquisition due diligence. Deal size and comfort level with the numbers provided by the seller are two determining factors.

In the introduction of this book we make reference to the purchase of an income property as sometimes feeling like a shotgun wedding. From the time an offer is made and accepted everything is in hurry up mode.

For those attempting to perpetrate a fraud this is a good thing, because buyers in a hurry make mistakes. Serious rent roll analysis requires the buyer to slow down and search for answers to pertinent questions about income. Forensic accounting requires even more time.

Accounting is the science of recording and reporting on financial transactions. These recordings all have a starting point. The starting point is usually the exchange of money for services rendered. You pay the electric company at the end of the month based on the services provided you, i.e., electricity for the most recent prior month. The invoice presented constitutes a transaction between you and the electric company. Payment of this invoice completes the transaction.

In forensic accounting you are looking for obvious variances from normal operational expectations. Sure, it would be nice to bring in the big guns and drill down to the penny, but most people buying a two million dollar deal are unlikely to chip in twenty grand for hard core forensic accounting.

The common sense methodology is to follow the paper trail matching seller–provided information with third–party, unbiased confirmation.

Tax bills, maintenance costs, rental income. Do these numbers as provided by the seller tie with documents provided by third party sources? Not always to the penny, of course, but generally?

If a seller represents that a certain service provider charges $1,011 monthly and you find the actual bill is $1,101 this is no time to gloat or make a call touting your triumphant investigative skills. The question that arises from your team is to determine if this is a repetitive pattern of behavior on the part of the seller. Are expense numbers, verified by third–party sources, consistently higher than those represented by the seller? If the answer is yes, then this brings into question any and all documentation presented by the seller. If some are higher and others lower (but close to actual), then intentional misrepresentation is less likely.

But here's the kicker: Everything can look perfect! I mean down to the penny perfect! Does this sound alarms? I hate to present a conspiracy theory, but yes, this can be a problem. A seller is cast with presenting a potential buyer with fact–based accounting. The seller is not charged with making sure you are aware of each and every occurrence around the asset. If a planned freeway is going in (on the 20–year plan) or 500 units are being built across the street (with permits pulled two years ago–but nothing is up so far), these market dynamics are up to you to identify.

Learning the facts about an asset pre–acquisition can be priceless if the conclusions lead you to reconsider the purchase based on findings. This is beyond negotiating price and terms. Consider that knowing the facts, the real facts prior to an acquisition, may lead you to eliminate an asset for cause—the cause being too many gaps in the information provided.

How do you apply forensic accounting to real estate investing? With investigative skills and a focused effort on fact finding. Getting to brass tacks, here are five things that you as an individual investor can do to implement some forensic accounting tactics.

- Review original documents. Example: You always want to review original leases. Check dates. Look for original and varied signatures from lease to lease. Look for consistency in terms of having in–place renewals.

- Cross–reference certain numbers with third party verifications. Example: Check with the county Recorder's office to confirm that the amount of real estate taxes paid reflected in the seller's documents corresponds with the amount due.

- Bank statements. As discussed prior, income on the rent roll should match deposits on bank statements. Example: When deposits on bank statements are higher than rental income, this amount should connect with ancillary income sources. Break down this amount to see if bank deposits above rental income tie with other income reported.

- Utility bills vary widely from place to place. Set aside personal biases and assumptions and spot check utility bills for the subject property against local use standards. Some buildings run on all electric, others have 50–year–old boilers. Inquire with local utilities to see what utilities apply to the property you're looking to purchase.

- Third–party contracts can vary wildly. Ask to review any contracts that seem unusually high or low. <u>Example</u>: Lawn care may be performed by a family member for $400 cash when charges from an arms–length service provider could reasonably be expected to cost double this amount.

Performing forensic accounting within the limited time available during the due diligence process can be expensive. However, it is far less costly than proceeding with a purchase blind, or partially blind, only to find out material facts after closing.

High–touch analysis brings you right into contact with relevant documents that can confirm information provided by the seller or their representatives. It is the absolute best method for validating seller–provided financial information. As discussed, the leases are the heart of the matter with respect to confirming contractual rental revenue expectations.

Chapter 8:
Key Factors in
Credit Quality

Everything we have discussed thus far leads us down a narrow path toward validating contractual rental income. Credit quality is yet another stepping stone to raising your comfort level that current income does indeed have a future!

Following are categories you can document that all have an impact on occupancy levels and therefore affect income. The reference to credit quality and the factors presented here refer to the credit quality of the income stream generated from the real estate asset, not from individual tenants. This is a not–so–subtle point. Granted, you can identify credit quality from the lease review, but the real "tell" is in knowing about turnover, lease renewals and renewal rates, collections, late fees and evictions activity.

Knowing this information tells you much about how the asset is being managed under current ownership. You can see what they are paying attention to (or not) and their level of pro–active involvement (if any). If I ask the manager what their annual turnover rate is and the response is a blank stare, then I know the question posed was an original thought to them. Knowing the answer to the categories in the chapter will provide you with a high degree of certainty about the quality of the income stream from a property.

I once had a professor who sold medical equipment to hospitals. He was a terrible salesman and knew he would soon be fired. Feeling sorry for himself, he took off the suit and tie and stopped making appointments with hospital administrators. His new wardrobe was scrubs. His new daytime home was in the hospital employee lounge. It was amazing the things he learned from talking with the folks who actually did the day–to–day work. After listening to "war stories," he began making appointments with administrators again. The "stories" he told the hospital administrators were chilling! It was like he worked there—he knew the weaknesses, like what equipment was past servicing dates, why and how long a surgical room had been closed, etc. His sales soared. It seems the administrators were more afraid of him continuing to hang out on the premises than they were in giving him the sale so he would move on.

Learn the answers to the following categories and it will be as if you already work at the property. Know all of the information from these categories and you may know more about the property than the current owner.

Turnover

While turnover is a nice catch phase, in this business...increases in turnover mean you are burning cash. From baseline data you can now determine turnover and inquire about the fate of the residents no longer on the roll. What became of them? Each person previously on the rent roll was a paying customer and we are very interested in their fate.

What happened that they are no longer a paying customer? Inquiring minds want to know! Very often, it is standard stuff (the usual suspects), like a job change or moving from the area, marriage, down–sizing, etc. For purposes of this analysis, assumption is a very bad word. You really do want to know.

Learning why people move to a property is easier than finding out why they moved out. Gaining fact–based information on why people moved can be difficult but it is a necessary task for gaining knowledge about how a particular asset is being operated by the current manage-ment and ownership. Review the rent roll and denote resident names that are on the rent roll in the current month as compared to those removed from the previous year. Inquire about why these tenants moved. Yes, this is tedious. But if the turnover number is a significant percentage we are looking for patterns in departures. This is a "not so obvious" tactic for determining if the reasoning for departures is the property, property management (perhaps a lack of maintenance) or some other cause. Maybe competitive properties are offering incen-tives not matched by the property you are looking to purchase. Perhaps there was a convenient bus stop nearby that has moved further away from the property. Inquire, inquire, and inquire.

How do you reduce turnover? With an earnest focus on lease renewals. Concessions at lease renewal are always less expensive than turnover expenditures. Be it carpet cleaning, painting an accent wall or a few new light fixtures, any of these require less cash than a full make–ready. Considering turnover expenditures and potential days vacant, a small concession at turnover is a bargain.

Lease Renewals

The straightest line to maintaining high occupancy in rental property is focusing consistent attention on renewing existing leases. Ignoring this makes maintaining full occupancy near impossible.

Renewals are the cornerstone of stable property operations. The renewal process starts anywhere from 60 to 90 days prior to lease expiration. What is the policy of current management? Can they tell you where they are on renewals for the current quarter? If not, why not? What concessions, if any, are being offered at renewal? Answers to these questions speak to the stability of future income as reflected on the rent roll.

The backbone of being prepared for make–ready work is in the lease renewal process. Lease renewals are your leading indicator to upcoming turnover, right? Without proactive renewals, it is impossible to prepare for pending turnover. Renewals cannot be taken for granted. Beginning the renewal process 60 to 90 days prior to the end of the lease term is becoming standard operating procedure and represents the best tool in estimating make–ready work.

Lease Renewal Rates (Resident Retention)

Lease renewal rates directly affect income stability. Consistently high turnover impacts income stability and expenditures associated with turnover; first from lost revenue due to vacancy, next from increases in costs associated with making the property ready for the next resident.

What is the year–over–year renewal rate? A number north of 75% is very good. High renewal rates convert to a low turnover rate. Low turnover converts to high gross margins and less turnover expenditures.

Regarding resident retention: Is current management ahead of the curve on renewals 60 to 90 days ahead of lease–end dates? Planning ahead makes for a higher probability of stabilized operations. If your lease file review determines that leases are substantially incomplete (read: not in–force) it is highly probable that resident retention is also in disarray.

Planning for renewals is a primary methodology for capturing rent growth and maintaining stable occupancy. The more advanced the better and 60 to 90 days is no longer an uncommon management planning time–line for contacting tenants about renewing their lease.

Utilize non–cash concessions at renewal. From restaurant gift cards to cleaning carpets and updating light fixtures and blinds, these are all potential concessions to consider at renewal. The concession offered should be less than the additional rent captured in the rental increase over the next 12–months.

Lease start dates/lease end dates

This is separate and distinct from renewals. This category says much about the potential of unlocking value. What is the average length of tenancy? Is it 12–months or twelve years? Nationally, turnover is 50% annually. Turnover is a NOI killer. Reducing turnover through retention increases cash flow.

Knowing average tenancy allows you to better estimate future revenue and revenue growth. It may drive your lender nuts during a refinance to reflect that your rental property has significantly lower operating costs than similar properties. You need to "paint the picture" by sharing that dollars other operators spend for turnover you have devoted to long–term capital expenditures. This not only strengthens the asset, but also bodes well for the lender knowing they have a loan with an owner consistently reinvest in the asset.

Collections Activity

In a perfect world, on the first of every month you will receive 100% of contractual rent due for that month. The reality is this seldom occurs. There is such variation in the timing of "collections" that many owners rely on a relative meaning. Here is a definition:

Collections refer to the funds received for rents due—funds received, and banked on behalf of the property owner.

Focusing on the rent roll, collections refers to rents received, and not any other category. What percentages of rents are collected as of the first of the month? What is this percentage as of the second and third of the month? Collections in the 90th percentile on the first of the month are representative of a high quality income stream.

When collections activity increases, there is an out–sized expense in terms of time necessary to collect monies due. At some point (determined by management), it is better to not renew the lease of certain residents rather than expend the time necessary to continue collections activity.

Late Fee Revenue

Late fees can be an indicator of future collections. This fee is a mechanism to enforce timely payment of rent. The real target inquiry in reviewing late fee revenue is to determine the quality of the underlying tenant base. Once late fees become consistently high, say, more than 3% of annual revenue, it becomes a red flag requiring deeper investigation. Are late fees confined to a particular set of residents or is it property–wide? Is enforcement of the late fee provision uniform? What is the quality of the credit underwriting standards for new residents?

Let's make a distinction here; resident selection criteria can change to assure a greater probability of rent collections. To use an easy example, if leasing standards require a certain credit score plus earned income of not less than three times the rental amount, then approving an applicant that is below this standard will reduce collected revenue and boost "booked" late fees. There is no winner in recording late fees never collected.

Are late fee collections enforced? Both parties, the property manager and resident, have agreed to the terms of the lease. The lease has a provision for payment of late fees. Adhere to the terms of the lease, and enforce the provision.

Late fees in C–class multifamily properties can represent as much as 10% of revenue. Of course, this is earned through increased time, energy and effort in collecting payments. As part of the lease, late fees must be enforced fairly and evenly. It's imperative not to play games or show favoritism from a legal, fairness or financial perspective.

Evictions Activity

Evictions are expensive and time consuming. Evictions activity is reduced with good resident screening. Having very succinct resident screening standards allows for cut and dried decisions on who is approved for occupancy. A good resident screening standard removes the gray area and allows management to provide clear responses to those approved and those rejected for tenancy.

Consider performing the following exercise: Determine how many evictions were performed each year going back two or three years. Determine how long each eviction process required in terms of days. Convert this to the number of days of lost revenue each year. Is evictions activity a significant cost in terms of lost revenue and legal fees expended? What was the end result for each eviction? Did the resident voluntarily move once served or was there action necessitating legal fees?

Consider utilizing this exercise on all of the assets in your portfolio. This may bring to light some previously unknown patterns. For example, it may be only four or five residents requiring one full day a month of management time for collections. Knowing this allows for crafting a remedy and better utilizing staff time.

Although the information gathering process for this segment of due diligence may seem daunting, remember that most of the data from this chapter is collected automatically when creating a rent roll for the property under consideration. Refer to your rent roll to ascertain the categories presented in this chapter.

Lease Term

Collected Rents

Stated Lease Rents

Chapter 9:
Rent Roll Triangle

Most income property is purchased with the intent to own it for a long period of time; five years, ten years, twenty years, etc. So while it is important to know the current income, it is equally if not more important to understand the viability of the asset and its income stream going forward.

Before you start a road trip you have to know where you are on the map. The Rent Roll Triangle™ (RRT) furnishes pinpoint accuracy as to where a property is in terms of financial performance, and identifies very quickly the areas of concern. With this information you can focus your attention on remedies that will have the greatest impact on strengthening the financial performance of your asset.

RRT identifies strengths and weakness. Once known, you can implement fixes to remedy problems and push positive financial outputs. It's not enough to know the areas of concern and leave them untouched. Is an uncashed check really money? Not until deposited and cleared, right? The same holds true with RRT; find the money, get the money, put it in the bank.

What is the Rent Roll Triangle?

The outcome obtained from RRT is a percentage of maximum rental income the asset can generate. Therefore, the higher the percentage the closer the asset is to operating at it's maximum financial potential. The Rent Roll Triangle™ (RRT) is a measure of rental income stability. It captures the relationship between stated lease rents (SLR), collected rents (CR), and the lease term (LT), and measures performance on a percentage scale from zero to one hundred with one hundred being perfected financial outputs for the asset in question. Although there are four variables we refer to this as a triangle because three of the measures are property specific. Gross Potential Rent is a market–wide measure.

Rent Roll Triangle (RRT) is a calculation. Analogous to the term "Iron Triangle," used by political scientists to describe the strong ties between Congress, Bureaucracy, and Interest Groups in the

United States in matters of policy, the RRT emphasizes the powerful interaction of gross potential rents, current, or stated rents (per the lease), collected rents (collections), and the terms of in–place leases (lease terms) in predicting strength of income.

The Rent Roll Triangle™ (RRT) is a simple mathematical calculation to measure the stability of rental income based on gross rent potential, stated lease rents, collections and lease term.

Rent Roll Triangle™ (RRT) solves the problem of estimating relative stability of income for a rental property. RRT represents a form of "sensitivity analysis" for rental property. RRT allows for comparisons amongst and between similar properties. Further scholarly study of RRT, I anticipate, will point you to an increased understanding of the relationship between the variables. I welcome debate on the viability of this measure and hope it stirs discussion on similar methodologies to capture the relationship between these variables.

With respect to rental income, RRT immediately points to actionable areas of concern.

Components of the Rent Roll Triangle (RRT) are: gross potential rents (GPR), stated lease rents (SLR rent per the terms of in–force lease), collected rents (CR) and term of tenancy (lease term or LT). The individual elements of RRT represent the four variables within the equation. While it seems we have discussed these precepts at length throughout this book, we now fold all four into a single equation.

RRT localizes rent income problems allowing operators to address the area of concern in real time.

Reaching the number generated by the RRT will create more questions. These questions will provide you with further insight as to the stability, or quality, of the rental income from the application of RRT to rental property. RRT is simply one more method of viewing an income–producing asset. Relying on any single number to determine value is short–sighted. I caution against overreliance on any one measure including RRT.

We will begin by presenting the entire equation then break down each part of the triangle. By the end of this chapter the math required will be simple enough to do with pencil, paper and a basic calculator. The work is in obtaining actual data for use in the equation. As they say, garbage in, garbage out, so the numbers collected for solving RRT must be accurate to the best of your ability.

With respect to rental income, RRT points to actionable areas of concern. RRT localizes rental income problems allowing you to identify issues in real time. How? By interlocking the four variables and highlighting the disparities between them. For example:

- By identifying a significant gap between Gross Potential Rent (GPR) and stated lease rents (SLR). If SLR is far below GPR one question to ask is if this differential is market–wide or property specific? If market–wide, then this knowledge allows you to form competitive concessions to compete more effectively.

- If SLR (actual rents per the lease) are well below GPR, then the issue might be simple mismanagement. Perhaps current management or ownership doesn't care. Perhaps rents are low because the property cannot effectively compete due to its current physical condition.

- Assuming collections are an issue, you know this is directly linked to resident underwriting.

- Identification of leases where residents are departing prior to their lease term expiring. This problem could relate to resident screening or how management handles maintenance. The problem could be that management has dozens of unanswered maintenance calls. Or, the issue could be a wildly competitive market with neighboring properties cannibalizing each other just to capture any incremental occupancy increases.

On the revenue side, narrowing the discussion to factors that most affect rental income allows you to cut to the problem area early in your review and see what's under the hood. Will the patient respond to treatment? Do you have the right team to administer treatment given your yield requirements and expertise? Do you want to perform this treatment or move on to another property with greater profit potential?

Building Blocks of RRT

We are about to discuss the variables of RRT at length. Some might think to the point of exhaustion. Knowing the variables backward and forward allows you freedom to devote precious due diligence time to other matters. Having this piece "down cold" you can drill down to items usually ignored or left to last because time is running out during the due diligence time you have remaining. Flounder here and you might miss an opportunity to see competitive assets, perform a 100% lease file review or skip the planned demographic analysis.

There are four components to creating and completing your analysis using RRT: gross potential rents, stated rental revenue per in–place leases, actual collections and lease term. One variable, gross potential rents, is obtained from the market where the property competes. The other three variables are specific to the asset in question. The triangle represents the three property specific variables.

- Gross Potential Rents (GPR – using real time market rental rates)

- Stated Lease Rent (SLR – stated rents per in–force leases)

- Collected Rent (CR – actual collections)

- Lease Term (LT – percent of lease term fulfilled)

Having read this book from beginning to end you will be familiar with this terminology. In this chapter is a synopsis on each component of RRT with a discussion of each term in detail as a preface to their use in RRT.

Although there are four variables we refer to this is a triangle because three of the measures are property specific. Gross Potential Rent is a market–wide measure.

Gross Potential Rents (GPR)

Gross Potential Rents (GPR) is a reflection of maximizing rents on a daily basis. GPR is a present day representation of current market rents. Regardless of in–place rents, GPR should be regularly updated to reflect current, real time, rental income potential. Consider that every vacant unit has as a price target which is the maximum market rent that can be obtained in a reasonable period of time. That highest price point may be adjusted daily. Like the price of a stock, if there are no buyers the price may adjust downward and if there are more buyers than sellers the price may adjust upward as demand increases. It is not a static number or one to get stuck on. GPR adjusts to market conditions.

Stated Lease Rent (SLR)

With rental property most tenants are paying in advance for services received over the next 30 days. Rent is due on the first of the month, to pay for the next 30 days of occupancy. For purposes of rent roll analysis you want to know how much is due, per the written contractual leases in–force, and how much was paid and when. Simple, right? It's really a time value of money equation, just crunched into thirty day increments.

Does the rental income as presented by the seller represent the same rental income as reflected in a review of in–place leases? Most revenue from rental property is derived from rents, of course. The number that has the most meaning is contractual rental income.

Collected Rents (CR)

The sustainability and success of a rental property is based on collections. Strong collections come from good resident screening and the implementation of a sound collections policy. Collections represent the culmination of everything you have provided to residents for the right to receive funds for services rendered. Consistently low collections spell disaster. The fastest way to fail is to have a lax collection policy.

Collected Rents represent money received, as a percentage of rent due, obtained for contractual rents.

Without collecting rents, all of the services you have provided fall to ashes. As only a portion of collections is profit, usually, the vast majority of collected revenue is paid out to various lenders, vendors and service providers so that you may have the right to retain the profit earned from having provided housing to your residents.

We presume a high level of collections means a high quality income stream. This is an over–simplification. It is true that a high level of "consistent collections" can infer a high quality income stream. Yet even if this is the case, maintaining this level of quality requires lease documentation to validate your "going forward" expectations. This is so very important because things change. Competition, market dynamics, local and national economic occurrences can create change in your operational dynamics.

Your collection expectations are that in–place leases and actual collections will be the same number. In the real world, these two seldom meet. There is invariably a disparity caused by a present day event; from late payers to those that decide to pay two months in advance to people that skip out altogether. There are changes to the billed amount (rental increases) with residents forgetting to include this in their current payment.

A collection report states the name and address of your proper-ty, the name or identifying code of your resident, the rent due, the date the rent is due and the date the rent was received. There is a difference between a collections report and a rent roll. As you have read throughout this book, a rent roll, correctly assembled, is a very distinctive document providing you with an array of information. A collections report conveys actual collections for a given period, usually a single month.

Lease Term (LT)

Putting it simply, a lease is a term rental agreement. One of the many moving parts of rental property is multiple leases. Every lease has a start date and an end date, an inception and an eventual expiration. The sole source of information for the remaining lease term is the lease itself and any in–force addendums that may extend the lease beyond its original lease term. In transient rental markets the lease, for many, is nothing other than a formality to gain entry to the dwelling. This type of resident fully intends to pay when they want and what they want irrespective of any contractual obligations.

Lease Term; the interval between the time a lease goes into effect and its expiration.

What is the average length of in–place leases...in months? Is it 8 months or 18 months? From personal experience I can say the most profitable property I have ever purchased had an annual turnover rate of less than 20% per year. The least profitable property I have ever purchased experienced a turnover rate of 60% per year. Turnover kills cash! These are two extreme examples but represent real life occurrences of having all on–site systems in order, and quality management yet a significant variance in financial outcomes based on turnover.

The number that matters most when attempting to determine current rental income is comparing the rental amount as represented by in–place leases against actual collections. What percentage of lease rents (per the in–places leases) is collected? The goal, always, is 100%. The reality is invariably less. While gaining this snapshot of accuracy is important there is significantly deeper meaning within a lease. Valuing a lease requires knowing:

- The amount of rent received (collections)

- The contract term (lease term and extensions)

- Payment history

This is the starting point for performing a lease abstract. With this information you can begin to determine the quality of the income stream in question.

Credit quality of a lease is determined by the pay history of the lessee. This history began prior to the payer's current lease. A review of the lease file (paper or electronic) will likely find a credit report, records related to payment while in tenancy and notices about late fee charges, if any. Is the resident fulfilling the terms of the lease with respect to length of lease?

What percentage of the tenant base can be described as adhering to the lease terms in full? Multiplying the response to this query by the entire resident population begins to paint a picture of credit quality; that is, comparing expected payments per the terms of in–place leases and the actual lease terms fulfilled.

By providing a competitive rental product you can anticipate a certain level of occupancy at all times (not 100% of course). The short duration of leases allows people to commit for a single year making the commitment palatable.

Rental property with the least turnover, meaning a property experiencing high lease renewals (or retention) will experience less turnover costs.

The importance of lease renewals cannot be overstated. There is a direct correlation between the number of residents that remain in place for an extended period and the profitability of the rental property.

Taking out "Occupancy"

Let's take a moment to answer a question about why it is that occupancy is not part of the equation? How can a mathematical formula about rental income provide valid outputs without using occupancy? The answer is that occupancy is accounted for when comparing GPR to collections. When there are HUGE percentage differentials between these variables you can assume that occupancy is a factor.

The second reason for excluding occupancy is that there are too many definitions. We have physical occupancy, economic occupancy and revenue numbers per unit, per square foot, etc. My underlying reasoning for excluding occupancy is because people already focus on occupancy. Including occupancy in the RRT calculation, I believe, gives this one variable too much weight thus effectively negating the interplay between the other selected variables. In other words; occupancy is too easy. By leaving out occupancy, I am asking you to delve deeper into the elasticity of the numbers.

Rent Roll Triangle – Theory (The Math)

Some will ask why "the math" is at the tail end of this chapter rather than right up front. The reasoning is because I want you to consider application of the equation versus getting lost in the numbers. Granted, that may seem a little backwards considering this book is all about "the numbers." But in this case, practicality dictates that you consider the calculations after an in–depth discussion of the power behind the numbers. Another more blatant reason is that any math seems to make many a person skip, or read around equations of any sort.

A word about basic math rules; remember to always perform multiplication or division before addition or subtraction.

Here is how RRT is calculated:

(Fig. 1) RRT (%) = (SLR ÷ GPR x 100)(CR ÷ SLR x 100)
$$(1 - [12 - LT] \div 12) \text{ X } 100)$$

$$= (SLR \div GPR)(CR \div SLR)(1 - [12\text{--}LT] \div 12) \text{ X } 100)$$

Or

$$= (CR \div GPR)(1) - ([12\text{--}LT] \div 12)(100)$$

Where: [ ] designates absolute value, so that any sign is always positive

$$0 \div 12 \text{ (or any other number)} = 0$$

Where "X" = multiplication and "÷" = division

And, where mathematical operations inside parentheses are completed first; then regular parentheses, then bold parentheses, then outside operations

Where: GPR = Gross Potential Rents

SLR = Stated Lease Rents

CR = Collected Rents

LT = Lease Term

Here is an explanation:

First, RRT is calculated using four factors that are both interlocking but that also can each independently affect the rent roll (Figure 1). For example, lease terms (LT) influences RRT directly, and it also influences both collections (CR) and Stated Lease Rents (SLR). As an obvious example, a lease term of 10 months reduces collected rent (CR) over the more ideal term of 12 months. These relationships are shown in Figure 1, and are expressed mathematically in the equation shown.

The outcome obtained from RRT is a percentage of maximum rental income the asset can generate. Therefore, the higher the percentage the closer the asset is to operating at its maximum potential.

The resulting RRT is expressed as a percentage. Percentage is a form of data that statisticians sometimes refer to as "normalized" in that it takes information from different scales and allows their comparison on a single scale. A familiar example of normalization is student grade point average, often given on a scale from 0 to 4. Here, a school will take grades from different teachers who range broadly in how they give grades, put the grades all on the same scale, and calculate a summary grade that is assigned to the student, say 3.4 GPA for a semester, year, or total time and classes at the school.

The summary GPA is used by other schools, (e. g., a university) to compare likelihood of success of students who are coming from different high schools in different parts of the country and, indeed, the world. While the university would be quick to point out that they understand the high schools vary widely in how the "normalized" GPAs are assigned, it at least gives an indication of how well one student may perform in the classroom as opposed to another.

And so it is with the RRT (%) and the effect of the variables on rental income. RRT (%) is not an absolute value. The RRT (%) of a rental property will always fall somewhere between 0% and 100%. Further, a unit with a GPR of 50 million dollars, and one with a GPR of 3 million dollar, may both be 78%.

The advantage of such normalization is that it allows you a comparison of rent potential between rental properties that have widely disparate values. A disadvantage is that the user needs to keep in mind that 78% of $50 million is a much different amount of money than 78% of $3 million. And, while the basis for assignment of an RRT (%) may differ widely between individual rental properties for many reasons, the RRT (%) does provide an indication of how well one rental property might perform as opposed to another.

RRT Base Case (Quantitative Perfection)

Following is the "base case" of the RRT calculation, whereas the rental property in question is operating at full potential. Please remember to always perform multiplication or division before addition or subtraction.

Where: Gross Potential Rent: GPR = $100,000

Stated Lease Rents: SLR = $100,000

Collected Rents: CR = $100,000

Lease Term: LT = 12

RRT (%) = (SLR ÷ GPR x 100)(CR ÷ SLR x 100)
(1 − [12 − LT] ÷ 12) x 100)

= (SLR ÷ GPR)(CR ÷ SLR)(1 − [12–LT] ÷ 12 X 100)

Or

RRT (%) = (100,000 ÷ 100,000 X 100)(100,000 ÷ 100,000 X 100)
(1 − [12 − 12] ÷ 12 X 100)

= (100,000 ÷ 100,000)(100,000 ÷ 100,000)(1 − [12–12] ÷ 100)

= (100%)(100%)(100%)

= 100.00%

Or

RRT (%) = A. (SLR ÷ GPR x 100) = 100%

B. (CR ÷ SLR x 100) = 100%

C. (1 − [12 − LT] ÷ 12) x 100) = 100%

= (100%)(100%)(100%)

= 100.00%

In the preceding calculations, the asset is fully rented with every available space leased at the highest current market rent with stated lease rent (SLR) equaling GPR. Further, occupancy is 100% with no days vacant.

In real life, I have yet to see an asset that operates at this level of financial superiority. The hotel industry has a good handle on this as they can "turn" their inventory and have it "made ready" on the same day. Even still, average hotel occupancy hovers around 65% annually. Thus, even though their inventory is ready to rock, aside from peak times there is significant vacancy.

In rental property, multifamily in particular, an annual occupancy rate of 90–95% is considered exceptional. Yet even at this level of occupancy you can measure "seepage" to income from deviations in rents from GPR, vacancy, collections and lease term.

RRT allows you to measure these variables and "attack" the area of concern between actual and superior financial performance. With the application of RRT you can immediately identify the gap between GPR and SLR, and examine leases to find those with the greatest distance from GPR. You may decide not to renew these particular leases, or you may decide that presenting residents with huge rental increases is worth the risk of move–outs given how much under the market current rents represent.

The same premise holds true with the relationship between SLR and CR. First, identify the gap between the amounts of money that the leases say you should be collecting and actual collections. With this in formation you can then task which leases are potentially problematic and aim your energies on those that detract from maximizing the financial goals of the asset.

Here is another example. Suppose a rental property has a GPR of $250,000, stated lease rents (SLR) of $225,000 and collected rent (CR) of $200,000, and an average lease term (LT) of ten months. Using the equation you calculate the RRT (%) as follows:

Where: Gross Potential Rent: GPR $= \$250,000$

Stated Lease Rents: SLR $= \$225,000$

Collected Rents: CR $= \$200,000$

Lease Term: LT $= 10$

RRT (%) = (SLR ÷ GPR x 100)(CR ÷ SLR x 100)
$\quad$ (1 − [12 − LT] ÷ 12) x 100)

$\quad$ = (SLR ÷ GPR)(CR ÷ SLR)(1 − [12–LT] ÷ 12 X 100)

RRT (%) = (225,000 ÷ 250000 x 100)(200,000 ÷ 225,000 x 100)
$\quad$ (1 − [12 − 10] ÷ 12) x 100)

$\quad$ = (225,000 ÷ 250,000)(200,000 ÷ 225,000)
$\quad$ (1 − [12 − 10] ÷ 12 x 100)

RRT (%) = (225000 ÷ 250,000 x 100)(200,000 ÷ 225,000 x 100)
$\quad$ (1 − [12 − 10] ÷ 12 x 100)

$\quad$ = (225,000 ÷ 250,000)(200,000 ÷ 225,000)
$\quad$ (1 − [12 − 10] ÷ 100)

$\quad$ = (90%)(89%)(83%)

$\quad$ = 66.48%

RRT (%) = A. (225,000 ÷ 250,000 x 100) = 90%

$\quad$ B. (200,000 ÷ 225,000 x 100) = 89%

$\quad$ C. (1 − [12 − 10] ÷ 12) x 100) = 83%

$\quad$ = (90%)(89%)(83%)

$\quad$ = 66.48%

This number is a reflection of the asset operating at 66.48% of its maximum rental income potential.

Chapter 10:
Rent Roll Triangle:
Case Studies

Four variables make up the data sets used in RRT, and here is an abridged definition of each variable.

Gross Potential Rent (GPR). GPR represents a perfect world whereas every rentable square foot is 100% occupied all the time with never a single day of vacancy for any reason. GPR also presumes 100% collections for the entire year.

Stated Lease Rent is the lessee's representation of rental income derived from an income–producing real estate asset. Now that you have devoted extensive on how to validate rental income. You know to review in–place leases to verify income on a per unit basis and to cross reference this against bank statements to confirm receipt of funds as represented on the rent roll. You also know sellers may add cash to the property bank account to assure these numbers balance, yet that is a difficult thing to do over an extended period of time.

Collected Rent refers to the funds received for rents due; funds received, obtained and banked on behalf of the property. Collected rent is money received, as a percentage of rent due, from contractual rental income for contractual rents.

Lease Term is the interval between the time a lease goes into effect and its expiration. You know that identifying the average length of tenancy is a significant determinant of tenant stability.

The following case studies are presented to wrap some realism around the theory. Each is a synopsis rather than a soup to nuts solution for the asset described. Note that RRT is inherently about rent and revenue numbers. RRT precludes factors related to the age of a property, its condition or location. RRT is a starting point to identify further actions necessary to remedy gaps on the revenue side of, equation for property operations.

Base Case

The base case presumes 100% attainment for each category where:

- The property is attaining 100% of GPR

- The property is collecting 100% of stated lease rents

- That collections equals 100% of stated lease rents

- That each in–place lease reaches full maturity of 12–months.

Following is the "base case" of the RRT calculation, whereas the rental property in question is operating at full potential. Please remember to always perform multiplication or division before addition or subtraction.

Gross Potential Rent: GPR $\quad = \$100,000$

Stated Lease Rents: SLR $\quad = \$100,000$

Collected Rents: CR $\qquad = \$100,000$

Lease Term: LT $\qquad\quad = 12$

$$RRT (\%) = (SLR \div GPR \times 100)(CR \div SLR \times 100)$$
$$(1 - [12 - LT] \div 12) \times 100)$$

$$= (SLR \div GPR)(CR \div SLR)(1 - [12–LT] \div 12 \times 100)$$

Or

$$RRT (\%) = (100{,}000 \div 100{,}000 \times 100)(100{,}000 \div 100{,}000 \times 100)$$
$$(1 - [12 - 12] \div 12 \times 100)$$

$$= (100{,}000 \div 100{,}000)(100{,}000 \div 100{,}000)(1 - [12–12] \div 100)$$

$$= (100\%)(100\%)(100\%)$$

$$= 100.00\%$$

RRT (%) = A. (SLR ÷ GPR x 100) = 100%

        B. (CR ÷ SLR x 100) = 100%

        C. (1 – [12 – LT] ÷ 12) x 100) = 100%

    =   (100%)(100%)(100%)

    =   100.00%

I know this is redundant, but in the calculation, please remember to always perform multiplication or division before addition or subtraction.

Now let's present some real world scenarios. Following are case studies with narratives that will provide you with an RRT based on diversity in RRT variables.

Scenario #1

Lets consider 300 multifamily apartment units where stated lease rents are at 90% of GPR with average rents of $900 per unit per month. The objective is to reach and maintain market rents. Remember that GPR is always a moving target as a gauges of market rents in real time while moving rental increases and setting prices on available units higher or lower according to changes in the marketplace.

Gross Potential Rent: GPR = $3,300,000

Stated Lease Rents: SLR = $3,000,000

Collected Rents: CR = $2,950,000

Lease Term: LT = 12 months

RRT (%) = (SLR ÷ GPR x 100)(CR ÷ SLR x 100)
(1 − [12 − LT] ÷ 12) x 100)

= (SLR ÷ GPR)(CR ÷ SLR)(1 − [12–LT] ÷ 12 X 100)

Or

RRT(%) = (3,000,000 ÷ 3,300,000 X 100)
(2,950,000 ÷ 3,000,000 X 100) (1 − [12 − 12] ÷ 12) X 100)

= (3,000,000 ÷ 3,300,000)(2,950,000 ÷ 3,000,000)
(1 − [12–12] ÷ 12 X 100)

Or

RRT(%) = (3,000,000 ÷ 3,300,000 X 100)
(2,950,000 ÷ 3,000,000 X 100) (1 − [12 − 12] ÷ 12 X 100)

= (3,000,000 ÷ 3,300,000)(2,950,,000 ÷ 3,000,000)
(1 − [12–12] ÷ 100)

= (91%)(98%)(100%)

= 89.18%

$$RRT(\%) = \text{A. } (3{,}000{,}000 \div 3{,}300{,}000 \times 100) = 91\%$$

$$\text{B. } (2{,}950{,}000 \div 3{,}000{,}000 \times 100) = 98\%$$

$$\text{C. } (1 - [12 - 12] \div 12) \times 100) = 100\%$$

$$= (91\%)(98\%)(100\%)$$

$$= 89.18\%$$

Given GPR and SLR, this asset is operating at almost 90% of its maximum financial potential. This is an excellent deal from an operational perspective. The property operator is doing a lot of things right and is paying attention to market rents and pacing "asking rents" with the market. Collections are running at 98% of SLR which is also excellent.

There are five units out of 300 delinquent. That tells us management is doing a good job in the resident selection process. The one area in need of improvement is average occupancy. There is a $300,000 gap between SLR rents and GPR. Further investigation is required to determine if this is from occupancy, stagnant in–place leases or competitive forces.

Scenario #2

Lets consider an eight–plex in an older neighborhood with significant competition all around.

Gross Potential Rent: GPR = $150,000

Stated Lease Rents: SLR   = $100,000

Collected Rents: CR   = $ 75,000

Lease Term: LT   = 11 months

RRT (%) = (SLR ÷ GPR x 100)(CR ÷ SLR x 100)
$\qquad$ (1 − [12 − LT] ÷ 12) x 100)

$\qquad$ = (SLR ÷ GPR)(CR ÷ SLR)(1 − [12–LT] ÷ 12 X 100)

$$\text{Or}$$

RRT (%) = (100,000 ÷ 150,000 x 100)(75,000 ÷ 100,000 x 100)
$\qquad$ (1 − [12 − 11] ÷ 12) x 100)

$\qquad$ = (100,000 ÷ 150,000)(75,000 ÷ 100,000)
$\qquad$ (1 − [12–10] ÷ 12 x 100)

$$\text{Or}$$

RRT (%) = (100,000 ÷ 150,000 x 100)(75,000 ÷ 100,000 x 100)
$\qquad$ (1 − [12 − 11] ÷ 12 x 100)

$\qquad$ = (100,000 ÷ 150,000)(75,000 ÷ 100,000)(1 − [12–11] ÷ 100)

$\qquad$ = (67%)(75%)(91%)

$\qquad$ = 45.73%

RRT (%) = A. $(100{,}000 \div 150{,}000 \times 100) = 67\%$

B. $(75{,}000 \div 100{,}000 \times 100) = 75\%$

C. $(1 - [12 - 11] \div 12) \times 100 = 91\%$

= $(67\%)(75\%)(91\%)$

= 45.73%

This eight–plex is renting with actual rents far below GPR. The first question that comes to mind is whether GPR is really $150,000. Are comparative properties that are in similar condition really renting that much higher than the subject? My gut is the person assigning GPR to this deal is making an incorrect assumption in that they believe the subject asset is competitive with other properties that are in significantly better physical condition. Either that, or this is a highly competitive market where everyone is just trying to gain occupancy by any means possible.

Perhaps a new competitor has come into the marketplace knocking everyone else to their knees. A new competitor can be a newly renovated property; one that can differentiate itself based on upgrades or newly installed amenities.

Another part of the negative spiral on this deal is collections which represent only 75% of stated rents. So regardless of occupancy, the residents occupying the property are paying only three dollars of four dollars due each month.

Overstating the obvious, a property in poor condition has lower rents. A property in this financial condition is attracting a tenant base with a history of slow or no pay. You will know with further due diligence.

Scenario #3

This 12 unit building in a major city has rents that pace well with market rents but always seems to have one or two residents that leave after a short stay, with occupancy well under 12–months. This occurrence affects the occupancy and collections numbers severely based on the small number of units. Let's plug in the numbers to measure financial stability.

Gross Rent Potential: GPR = $345,600

Stated Lease Rents: SLR = $280,000

Collected Rents: CR   = $241,000

Lease Term: LT   = 10 months

RRT (%) = (SLR ÷ GPR x 100)(CR ÷ SLR x 100)
(1 – [12 – LT] ÷ 12) x 100)

= (SLR ÷ GPR)(CR ÷ SLR)(1 – [12–LT] ÷ 12 X 100)

Or

RRT (%) = (280,000 ÷ 345,600 x 100)(241,000 ÷ 280,000 x 100)
(1 – [12 – 10] ÷ 12) x 100)

= (280,000 ÷ 345,600)(241,000 ÷ 280,000)
(1 – [12–LT] ÷ 12 x 100)

Or

RRT (%) = (280,000 ÷ 345,600 x 100)(241,000 ÷ 280,000 x 100)
(1 – [12 – 10] ÷ 12 x 100)

= (280,000 ÷ 345,600)(241,000 ÷ 280,000)(1 – [12–10] ÷ 100)

= (81%)(86%)(83%)

= 57.88%

RRT (%)= A. (280,000 ÷ 345,600 x 100) = 81%

    B. (241,000 ÷ 280,000 x 100) = 86%

    C. (1 – [12 – 10] ÷ 12) x 100) = 83%

    =   (81%)(86%)(83%)

    =   57.88%

The inferences you can make from these numbers begins with the gap from GPR to CR; that's a big number! The lease term being so short tells you that many of the occupants are newer residents. Here is the big issue: It looks like there are many brand new residents and... you also have a collections problem with collected rents (CR) being $3,250 a month less than stated lease rents (SLR). That is an issue with resident screening. The property operator must step up collections and begin to reduce the number of non–paying residents with better resident screening.

Conclusion

Thank you for taking a journey with me through this guide to understanding rental income. I hope you have found it to be interesting, informative and sometimes thought provoking. The thinking behind this book is to equip the rental property buyer with tools to get ahead of the process given the time constraints allotted due diligence when buying property. Further, I hope those of you that own rental property will apply the metrics found here as a method of better understanding the assets you own.

Rental property ownership is a business in constant flux. Add to this that no two properties are the same and we have a lot of moving pieces to monitor. Using the formulas you have learned here will bring some consistency to the numbers and increase your comfort level in the decisions made knowing that sometimes the best decision is to walk away from a transaction with one too many problems. And when you find a jewel you will know it!

Please stay in touch. You can always find me blogging about all things multifamily at www.multifamilyinsight.net. For an invitation to upcoming podcasts on How to Read a Rent Roll and an opportunity to participate in free webinars covering each chapter of the book, please send an email to wecare@rentrolltriangle.com.

Resources

Following is resource material from my blog, Multifamily Insight (www. multifamilyinsight.net). I selected these particular resources because they deliver a lot of value in a small space. Whereas our entire blog can be considered a great resource on practical and operational matters related to multifamily, the information here can be implemented real time.

Following is list of powerhouse websites related to multifamily. Next is a list of property management mistakes to avoid. Then, our most popular blog post of all time: "Property Management—Nine Things Not in the Textbooks." Next is an article entitled, "The Three P's in Multifamily: People, Property and Paper." You have to know how these interact to get any deal done. The last article is, "Growing Revenue in Multifamily: The Ten Percent Rule." I consider this apropos as this book is all about analyzing income; so let's end on a high note and talk a little about growing income!

Websites

There are many websites focused exclusively on income–producing real estate. The purpose of this list of multifamily websites is to highlight those providing solid, current, quality content.

Some of the websites are regional, some global. Some are exclusively multifamily while others only have multifamily as part of the greater real estate asset class. All can add to your knowledge base about the multifamily business.

PREA (Pension Real Estate Association) is the best example. They allow us mere mortals access to current research papers written by Masters and PhD candidates supported by their organization and members. We thank them for this glimpse into the future of real estate.

1. **(PREA) Pension Real Estate Association.** The Pension Real Estate Association is a non–profit trade association for the global institutional real estate investment industry. To access current research

reports, select the Research and Market Information tab. Then select Real Estate Research Institute.

2. **Multifamily Executive.** Provides apartment executives with apartment and condo industry news, multifamily design ideas and apartment technology information.

3. **Units Magazine.** A publication featuring news and news makers in the multifamily housing industry. Features include interviews of members and topical articles about multifamily property management and ownership.

4. **IREM.** Institute of Real Estate Management. This property management mega–site offers more than just information on professional designations. IREM is an affiliate of the National Association of Realtors.

5. **MIT Center for Real Estate.** Provides information covering national and global trends in real estate including multifamily that touch on subjects from global capital flows to sustainability.

6. **Multifamily Biz.** A multifamily portal providing blogs and real–time industry specific news feeds, including information on nationwide multifamily conferences, products and trends.

7. **PowerHour Webcast.** Providing free hour–long web casts on topics specific to the multifamily industry.

8. **Real Estate Center at Texas A&M University.** All things "Texas" real estate including multifamily. Very detailed for the state but also has databases covering the nation.

9. **USC Lusk Center for Real Estate.** High quality data with statistical information related to southern California. Covers all real estate asset classes including multifamily.

10. **Multifamily Insight.** A website for owners, operators and investors in multifamily real estate. Provides content specific to the multifamily marketplace and free white papers on subjects specific to

the industry. Go to Free White Papers to see the list of available reports. There are additional free reports under the software tab.

Software

There is a multitude of software available for creating and tracking your rent rolls. Most are for use post–acquisition to deploy for on–going property management. The names are familiar: Yardi, AppFolio, etc. Through a service provided by Software Advice, they provide recommendations based on your presented needs for property management. Multifamily Insight does have an affiliate relationship with this company. You can find their material on our website along with White Papers about selecting property management software.

Unfortunately, there are few offerings for rent roll analysis. PRO–APOD is one software that has a good track record and can easily assist the under $5M buyer in assessing income property.

For financial analysis another software program I like is offered by Real Data (www.realdata.com) by Frank Gallinelli.

Property Management Mistakes

A real estate investor is not necessarily a real estate property manager, right? If the following mistakes are occurring with the assets under consideration for purchase, after closing is the time to install new management, first to stop the damage and second to remedy the potential of on–going issues and the legal exposure they present.

1. Allowing a danger to public safety to persist. Suspect electrical, known illegal drug use, endangerment of children, domestic abuse, and violent behavior. No good choices here. All or any similar issues must be addressed in real time once known.

2. Creating, encouraging or allowing fraudulent acts. No skimming off the top. Property mangement is a business. If you find providing service with high levels of integrity is hard, then get out of the business, please.

3. Keeping a bad hire. Other than fire or natural disasters, keeping a bad hire is one of the costliest mistakes. It is one thing to make the mistake, quite another to allow it to persist and potentially cause more damage.

4. Bad resident screening (or no resident screening). Anymore, the expense of obtaining a background screening is really, really cheap insurance. Having this tool available and failing to implement it is trouble waiting to happen.

5. Letting water run. Indoors or out, running water is seldom a positive. Find the pliers. Call the plumber, the roofer, the candle stick maker– whoever has the answer. Get that water stopped the same day or hour!

6. Allowing insurance to lapse. Murphy's Law lives here.

7. Ignoring maintenance requests. News flash...they do not go away. Goodwill is hard to earn, easy to lose. If you do not care about your tenants who will?

8. Ignoring renewals. The number one objective to retaining a stable income stream is making sure your tenants renew their leases. This requires a proactive renewal policy. No renewals policy, no stable income.

9. Lack of recordkeeping. Uncle Sam eventually catches up and when he does it's like an ocean wave hitting a single piece of sand. Keep good records, and file tax documents on time using quality service providers.

10. The telephone. There are varying policies regarding telephone etiquette and responsiveness. Implement a policy and stick with it. Your tenants and potential tenants want consistency. Having the attitude of "they'll call back" is self–deception. "They" (potential tenants) do not. They talk to the next person who picks up the phone, possibly your competition.

Property Management: 9 Things Not in the Textbooks

In property management I believe many of the points presented in this book will be true five years from now. Like the chart of a long–term investment, (one day does not a portfolio trend make.) The same holds true in property management.

The property management business will never be any less complex than it is today. Imagine that you lose your cell phone and it cannot be replaced for a week. In the interim there's an "old" phone in the drawer...that's five years old. The effort it would take to remember how it works may outweigh the effort to use it...if it would even work on today's networks.

Here are some things I believe hold true over the long run:

Property presentation is imperative. Property presentation is your visual contact with current and potential tenants. When looking at your property, try to see what your tenants see and ask yourself if that initial impression would be positive or negative. Work on the negatives, accentuate the positives.

Management training is important, and there is such a thing as too much training. There must be "spacing" (read: time) between training to allow for implementation of new procedures/processes.

Landscaping is an asset. In an effort to reduce costs, this aspect of a property is often reduced towards extinction. However, removing all landscaping from all buildings is like removing its character, making them all the same. How boring is that?

Controlling utility expenses must continue to be a focal point of every proactive property management company. Not only does it save real dollars, it also provides job security as increased cash flow can give a cushion for keeping/continuing with professional management.

Relationships are key to any established business. The same is true in the multifamily business. With established relationships in place, you can focus on G.R.A.C.E growing revenue and controlling expenses.

The ancillary income category will continue to expand as our industry derives additional service categories. Look to services being offered by hotels and extended, stay hotels for clues as to what may be coming next in the multifamily industry. The industry is not quite at the point of offering "bedding turn down service"...but it could happen.

Innovation begins in our 24–hour cities and spreads outward. Innovation often begins with the solving of a problem. In fast–paced, high population cities, problem solving for a tenant concern or request has many minds working on the same problem. How many properties had wireless Internet ten years ago? If the "fix" has legs, then this same solution spreads throughout a property and then to other properties. This same innovation will spread to other big cities and then throughout the country.

Commodity costs continue to rise (wood, metal, fabric, paint). Be selective with installed fixtures to assure they have "timelessness" to them. Override trendy with traditional colors. It's one thing to have a "hip" leasing office, but inside units, traditional colors and finishes provide extended life and more value to owners.

Three P's of Multifamily: People, Property and Paper

Every successful owner of a multifamily property must deal with the "Three P's" of real estate in a proactive manner. They are; people, property and paper. Real estate investing requires expertise in all three categories. Following are examples that fit into each category. This is by no means an all–inclusive list, just a sample of items that impact the value of your property.

People. Every business is built on relationships and the multifamily business is no different.

Customer contact. Who is the public representative of your property? Who is the first person a tenant meets when considering your property as their residence? Are they representing you well? I remember reading about the CEO of Avis having an eye–opening experience when calling his own company to rent a car. Not all was well on the home front.

Maintenance. Is maintenance not only responsive but respectful? There is more to customer service that just fixing the issue. Along with promptness, courtesy always goes a long way.

Vendors. Can you call a plumber at 5:01 p.m. and not get hit up with an after–hour charge? What is your relationship with your vendors? Take the time to get to know when their slow season is and hire them during those times. This will go a long way to get you closer to the top of the list when you need a fast turn.

Banking. This industry has changed dramatically in recent times but do not discount the need to have a working relationship with your bank. Do you have a "go to" person for not just loans but everyday banking services? Is there more than one person at the main branch who knows your name?

Property. What is the first impression and lasting impression your property presents to current and future customers?

> **Management.** Are your management systems in place and being followed?
>
> No unit is ready for showing until its ready. No shortcuts here. You only get one chance to make a first impression.
>
> Is landscaping in good order and trash picked up?
>
> If the pool it open is must be sparkling and ready for use.

Paper. Paper represents the documents that secure your ownership position. Without it, there is no "paper trail" to prove to anyone your right to the income stream created by the asset.

Ownership documentation.

Ownership structure.

Financing. Bank loans and other financing documents.

Insurance. Is your insurance in order and up–to–date? Do you have emergency phone numbers for weekend emergencies? Hail and wind damage does not wait until Monday to be addressed. Does your manager have a camera on hand to take immediate photos of an occurrence?

Growing Revenue in Multifamily: The 10% Rule

Often in a given marketplace competitive properties have many similarities. Granted, they may not have the same look or facade, but rent rates are similar (revenue per square foot of occupied space, for example); amenities are similar; they are the same distance from job centers or shopping, etc. A deeper look will often reveal that tenants are coming from the same pool; tenants have similar job titles, educational levels and credit scores. Same, same and more of the same. The 10% Rule proposed here is not an exercise to keep management busy or to assuage any particular interest group. The objective is to increase occupancy, and not just through the continued use of concessions.

The 10% rule states that you will consider any single change from the norm in up to ten percent of the units in a development.

The following examples assume 100 units or more and that not more than ten units in total are "in play" to unconventional offers. The objective is to fill vacant units, not change the character or viability of the property. Here are some examples of how to apply the 10% Rule:

Demographics. For starters; expand your demographic. Again, not by lowering screening standards, but through identifying additional people who fit your tenant profile. This may mean expanding advertising into channels that were previously ignored. A simple example is posting brochures in senior citizen and community centers. This demographic is more transitional than ever before; and they have income. Some sell homes and move to apartments close to where they have lived for many years. Many are looking to downsize but not leave their long–time neighborhood. Not everyone over the age of fifty is going straight to assisted living. Baby Boomers are active in their community and they have income!

Short–term leases. Most operators have no interest in short–term leases due to the increased turnover costs. However, when vacancy is persistent, consider offering a few units with short–term leases at a 10% premium to asking rents.

Utilities paid. A quick review of utilities history will tell you the average cost per month for utilities (electric, gas) on a specific unit size. Offer a single unit with "utilities paid" and adjust the rental asking price accordingly. Do not in any way lower your screening processes to fill this unit.

Free cable and Internet. On a per unit basis, offer one or two units with "free cable and internet." For many properties this is standard already but for many others it is not. In many cases either the entire property is wired or it is not. Similar to other utilities, the cost for providing this service for one unit is very easy to determine. Consider it a loss leader that may assist in filling one or two additional units. Likely, over one year, the cost will be similar to one month free rent, but note the concession is granted over the term of the lease.

Furnished units. Get quotes in advance from Aaron's Rents or similar vendors for the cost to furnish an apartment with living room, dining room and bedroom furniture only. Corporate rentals would require full kitchen and linens. Just stick to offering the furnishings only and perhaps a television.

Subsidized rents. Most individuals and families that have vouchers are good people. Even if you have not previously considered accepting HUD vouchers, consider doing so. There are thousands of families and people of retirement age looking for housing that have a voucher and cannot find a property to accept their money. This in no way implies changing your screening standards. It will require having an inspection and filling out more paperwork than usual for a single lease but accomplishes a public good concurrent with decreasing your vacancy. A win/win.

The objective is, on a continuous basis, to increase rents and revenue while providing the highest quality competitive products to your tenants. On that note, be prepared to step outside of your comfort level. Management's best efforts to garner increases in occupancy may not manufacture positive results. So try some new methods! Unconventional ways, a little different, a little quirky! As noted earlier, as everyone is continuing to target the same pool of tenants in the same way, so you need to be willing to step outside of the usual box.

Index

A

B

C

D

E

F

G

H

L

Late Fees 18, 57, 69, 72, 73, 109, 113, 114
Lease 10, 11, 18, 19, 20, 22, 24, 25, 33, 47, 51, 52, 64, 72, 73, 80, 81, 82, 84, 93, 94,
     95, 100, 102, 105, 109, 111, 112, 113, 114, 135, 136, 138, 143, 153, 154, 168
Lease File Review vi, 93
Lease Renewal Rates vii, 111
Lease Renewals 82, 109, 111
Lease Rent 62, 135
Leases i, 10, 17, 18, 19, 20, 21, 26, 33, 51, 58, 80, 81, 82, 93, 95, 105, 111, 135, 139,
     153, 168
Lease Term 11, 18, 64, 73, 81, 95, 111, 143

M

Magic Number #1 v, 48
Magic Number #2 v, 49
Market Rent 33, 34, 37, 123, 131
Misrepresentation vi, 101

N

NOI 2, 10, 49, 50, 52, 53, 57, 112, 164

R

Renewals 82, 94, 105, 109, 111, 112, 148
Rent i, ii, 1, 2, 3, 5, 6, 7, 8, 9, 10, 11, 15, 16, 17, 18, 19, 20, 21, 22, 23, 24, 25, 26, 30,
     31, 32, 33, 34, 36, 37, 46, 48, 49, 50, 51, 53, 54, 57, 58, 59, 60, 61, 62, 63, 64,
     65, 69, 70, 72, 73, 80, 81, 82, 83, 87, 94, 95, 96, 97, 101, 102, 104, 105, 110,
     111, 112, 113, 115, 135, 147, 151, 152, 153
Rental Income 2, 5, 6, 9, 10, 11, 15, 16, 17, 18, 19, 20, 21, 22, 26, 33, 47, 48, 49, 50,
     58, 69, 72, 76, 80, 82, 85, 87, 94, 95, 102, 104, 105, 109, 135
Rental Property 2, 5, 6, 15, 16, 17, 23, 26, 29, 30, 38, 40, 45, 52, 53, 54, 63, 72, 73,
     74, 76, 79, 81, 84, 96, 100, 112, 114, 136
Rent Per Square Foot 36, 60, 61
Rent Per Unit 62, 63
Rent Roll i, ii, 1, 2, 3, 5, 6, 7, 9, 10, 11, 17, 18, 19, 20, 21, 22, 23, 24, 25, 26, 33, 36,
     46, 48, 49, 50, 51, 53, 58, 60, 64, 69, 70, 80, 81, 82, 83, 87, 94, 95, 96, 97,
     101, 104, 105, 110, 111, 113, 115, 135, 147
Rent Roll Triangle v, vii, 3, 13, 117, 133
Revenue i, v, vi, vii, 2, 3, 5, 6, 9, 10, 15, 17, 18, 21, 24, 26, 29, 34, 43, 45, 46, 47, 48,
     49, 50, 52, 53, 54, 57, 59, 60, 61, 63, 65, 67, 69, 70, 71, 72, 73, 74, 77, 80, 84,
     86, 93, 96, 98, 111, 112, 113, 114, 135, 145, 150, 152, 154, 164, 167, 168
Revenue Per Square Foot vi, 70
Revenue per Unit vi, 71
RRT vii, 11, 135, 136, 137, 138, 140, 142

S

T

U

Free E–books

Type the link below into your Internet browser to get your free e–book today!

http://www.multifamilyinsight.com/white–papers/

For a podcast invitation from the author of How to Read a Rent Roll and an opportunity to participate in free webcasts covering each chapter of the book, please send an email to wecare@rentrolltriangle. com. Each of our podcasts and webcasts are focused on giving you the tools, resources and strategies to read a rent roll with the expertise only available to industry insiders.

Multifamily Insight is John Wilhoit's website providing his "insight" into the world of multifamily acquisitions, management and investing. To subscribe to his blog go to: www.multifamilyinsight.com. WIN LLC is based in Columbia, MO at 573–886–8992 or visit their website and www.win–rei.com

Additional contact information for the author:

Email: wecare@rentrolltriangle.com

Twitter: www.twitter.com/johnwilhoitjr

LinkedIn: www.linkedin.com/in/johnwilhoit

For information on author speaking engagements or bulk book sales, please contact WIN Publishing at Info@win–rei.com.

John Wilhoit, Jr.

MAKE MONEY. BUILD WEALTH.

Market Analysis

Multi-family Acquisitions

Property Management

Real Estate Finance

MULTIFAMILY INSIGHT VOL. 1

How to Build Wealth Through Buying the Right
Multifamily Assets in the Right Markets

MultifamilyInsight.com

AVAILABLE NOW
ON AMAZON!

John Wilhoit, Jr.

RENT
ROLL
TRIANGLE

RentRollTriangle.com

COMING IN 2014!

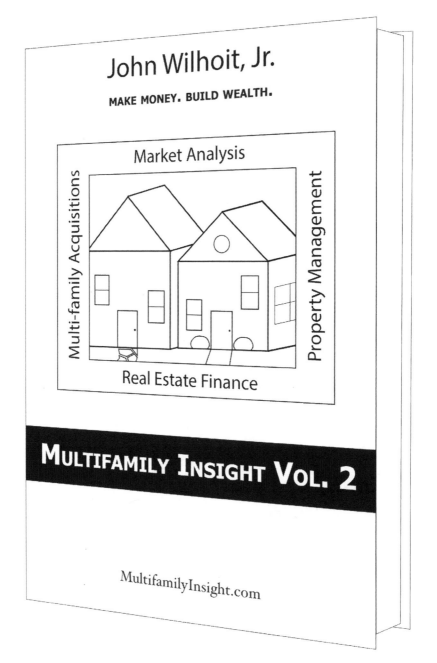

COMING IN 2014!

Ernest F. Oriente, a business coach and trainer since 1995, and a property management industry professional since 1988——is the author of SmartMatch Alliances...the founder of PowerHour®, PowerHourSEO™, PowerHourSales Academy™, PowerHour Leadership Academy™ and Power Insurance & Risk Management™, has a passion for coaching his clients on executive leadership, hiring and motivating property management SuperStars, traditional and Internet SEO/SEM marketing, acquisitions, competitive sales strategies, and high leverage alliances for property management teams and their leaders.

He and his PowerHour® team provide private and group coaching for property management companies around the world, executive recruiting, investment banking, real estate and apartment building insurance, SEO/SEM web strategies, national WiFi solutions, employee policy manuals, social media leadership and powerful tools for hiring property management SuperStars and building dynamic teams.

PowerHour® runs the largest 19 LinkedIn groups in the world for property management success called Property Management Professionals and has created Wikipedia for the property management industry, www.powerhour.com/propertymanagement/linkedingroups.html

Since 1995, Ernest has written 200+ articles for the property management industry and created 350+ property management forms, business and marketing checklists, sales letters and presentation tools. To subscribe to his free property management newsletter go to: www.powerhour.com. PowerHour® is based in Olympic–town, Park City, Utah, at 435.615.8486 or visit their website: www.powerhour.com

Ernest F. Oriente, a business coach and trainer since 1995, and a property management industry professional since 1988——and John Wilhoit, Managing Member of WIN LLC, 20+ year multifamily owner and asset manager of apartments, condominiums and townhomes, are the co–founders of PowerHour Leadership Academy Power.

Join our weekly PowerHour Leadership Academy www.powerhourleadershipacademy.com/pm] for leaders who want to increase their fees, expand their new business development while controlling expenses that will maximize their NOI plus increase the net worth of their company...with a focus on GRACE [Grow Revenue & Control Expenses].

Our working together is focused on the areas below and is available for only one property management company per city:

Grow Your Revenue...showing you 15 ways to gain more revenue, increase your new client relationships and grow your market share/impact

Direct Competitors...working together on a 13–part presentation focused on how to out–sell and out–market those you are competing most with

Your Team...focusing on interviewing skills, hiring best–practices, compensation plans, and the steps for training and retaining the very best

Control Expenses...with discussions related to bids/RFPs, vendor selection and compliance and best–practices from an expert vendor/supplier perspective

Your industry coaches have:

- 88+ years of combined expertise in the property management sector

- Asset management of $300 million in portfolio equity

- Asset management of 7 state region with 6,500 units and 35% in the construction phase

- Asset management for publicly–held REIT overseeing a portfolio of 2,800 units in 16 states

- Asset management of 186 LIHTC properties with $150 million in portfolio equity

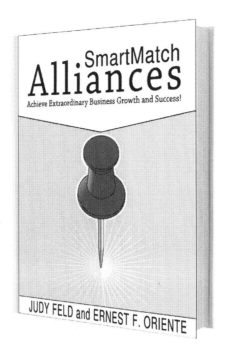

Ernest F. Oriente, a business coach and trainer since 1995, and a property management industry professional since 1988——is the author of SmartMatch Alliances™ The founder of PowerHour®, PowerHour SEO™, PowerHour Sales Academy™, PowerHour Leadership Academy™ and Power Insurance & Risk Management™. When you enter the world of SmartMatch Alliances™ you will open the door to extraordinary business growth and success.

Learn how you can quickly:

- Charge more for your property management rentals, earn more and have more fun!

- Attract better business prospects for your property management company – in greater numbers – faster than ever before!

- Learn a no–nonsense process for maximizing your alliance results!

- Break through the clutter and attract more property management opportunities, new revenue streams, and prospects than you've ever imagined!

- Learn from like–minded people and companies in the property management industry!

- Establish a strong, memorable brand for yourself, your property management company and your rental housing inventory/options!

- Create a business–building strategy that's low– to no–risk and always win–win – one in which the only limits are your own imagination, creativity, and energy!

Since 1995, Ernest has written 200+ articles for the property management industry and created 350+ property management forms, business and marketing checklists, sales letters and presentation tools. To subscribe to his free property management newsletter go to: www.powerhour.com. PowerHour® is based in Olympic–town, Park City, Utah, at 435.615.8486 or visit their website: www.powerhour.com

365connect
PLATFORM DRIVEN TECHNOLOGY

Award–winning *365 Connect* was founded in 2003 by a team of multifamily housing professionals with the primary goal of maximizing and accelerating online activities that reduce costs and increase revenue in the multifamily marketplace. Committed to delivering innovative solutions to meet the rapidly changing needs of the multifamily housing industry, *365 Connect* is the industry leader in designing and delivering an array of online platforms that work in unison with each other to market, lease and retain residents in multifamily communities.

What makes *365 Connect* different? *365 Connect* resolves issues every multifamily community faces: marketing, online leasing, managing social media, and delivering services to residents to keep them renewing leases. The *365 Connect Platform* has the ability to market communities across the Internet to high traffic sites, automate social media postings and deliver desktop and mobile platforms for prospects to transact business. It follows the entire resident lifecycle and delivers services after the lease is signed. By providing residents with a content rich platform laced with online services and communication tools, the *365 Connect Platform* strives to enhance retention rates.

Explore: www.365connect.com

multifamilybiz.com

MultifamilyBiz.com is the Next Generation Internet Platform for the Multifamily Industry and is the place to be for everything touching multifamily housing. *MultifamilyBiz.com* covers the entire spectrum of multifamily housing, including market–rate, affordable, student and senior housing, in both the rental and for sale markets. From the latest industry news, member posted press releases, to its robust vendor directories, *MultifamilyBiz.com* is dedicated to providing a suite of focused, leading–edge, online tools and resources designed to maximize and accelerate commercial activities in the multifamily marketplace.

The vision of the *MultifamilyBiz.com* is to build an arena where its members play an active part in the evolution of the site through building and creating content, posting press releases, sponsoring webcast, uploading video and designing new resources and tools. To effectuate that vision, *MultifamilyBiz.com* is designed to drive multifamily businesses and technology into a focused marketplace to maximize efficiency and creativity across the multifamily industry.

MultifamilyBiz.com is a powerful interactive and dynamic hub that has emerged as one of the largest websites of its kind in the multifamily housing industry. It drives multifamily enterprises, personnel, assets and technology into a focused community and marketplace. *MultifamilyBiz.com* has created the ultimate platform for businesses and communities to share their products and services directly with the multifamily housing industry.

Explore: *www.MultifamilyBiz.com*

Made in the USA
Lexington, KY
17 December 2017